Maths

Assessment Papers
Challenge

9–10 years

Great Clarendon Street, Oxford, OX2 6DP, United Kingdom

Oxford University Press is a department of the University of Oxford.
It furthers the University's objective of excellence in research, scholarship,
and education by publishing worldwide. Oxford is a registered trade mark of
Oxford University Press in the UK and in certain other countries

Text © Paul Broadbent 2015
Illustrations © Oxford University Press 2015

The moral rights of the authors have been asserted

First published in 2015
This edition published in 2021

All rights reserved. No part of this publication may be reproduced,
stored in a retrieval system, or transmitted, in any form or by any
means, without the prior permission in writing of Oxford University
Press, or as expressly permitted by law, by licence or under terms
agreed with the appropriate reprographics rights organization.
Enquiries concerning reproduction outside the scope of the above
should be sent to the Rights Department, Oxford University Press, at
the address above.

You must not circulate this work in any other form and you must
impose this same condition on any acquirer

British Library Cataloguing in Publication Data
Data available

978-0-19-277821-5

10 9 8 7 6 5 4

Paper used in the production of this book is a natural, recyclable
product made from wood grown in sustainable forests.
The manufacturing process conforms to the environmental
regulations of the country of origin.

Printed in China

Acknowledgements

The Publishers would like to thank Michellejoy Hughes for her
contribution to this edition.

The publishers would like to thank the following for permissions
to use copyright material:

Page make-up: GreenGate Publishing Services, Tonbridge, Kent
Illustrations: GreenGate Publishing Services, Tonbridge, Kent
Cover illustrations: Lo Cole

Although we have made every effort to trace and contact all
copyright holders before publication this has not been possible in all
cases. If notified, the publisher will rectify any errors or omissions at
the earliest opportunity.

Links to third party websites are provided by Oxford in good faith
and for information only. Oxford disclaims any responsibility for
the materials contained in any third party website referenced in
this work.

The manufacturer's authorised representative in the EU for
product safety is Oxford University Press España S.A. of El Parque
Empresarial San Fernando de Henares, Avenida de Castilla, 2 –
28830 Madrid (www.oup.es/en or product.safety@oup.com).
OUP España S.A. also acts as importer into Spain of products
made by the manufacturer.

Introduction

What is Bond?

The Bond *Challenge* titles are the most stretching of the Bond assessment papers, the number one series for the 11+, selective exams and general practice. Bond *Challenge* is carefully designed to stretch above and beyond the level provided in the regular Bond assessment range.

How does this book work?

The book contains two distinct sets of papers, along with full answers and a Progress Chart:

- Focus tests, accompanied by advice and directions, are focused on particular (and age-appropriate) maths question types encountered in the 11+ and other exams, but devised at a higher level than the standard *Assessment Papers*. Each Focus test is designed to help raise a child's skills in the question type as well as offer plenty of practice for the necessary techniques.

- Mixed papers are full-length tests containing a full range of maths question types. These are designed to provide rigorous practice for children working at a level higher than that required to pass the 11+ and other maths tests.

Full answers are provided for both types of test in the middle of the book.

Some questions may require a ruler or protractor. Calculators are not permitted.

How much time should the tests take?

The tests are for practice and to reinforce learning, and you may wish to test exam techniques and working to a set time limit. We would recommend your child spends 55 minutes answering the 50 questions in each Mixed paper.

You can reduce the suggested time by five minutes to practise working at speed.

Using the Progress Chart

The Progress Chart can be used to track Focus test and Mixed paper results over time to monitor how well your child is doing and identify any repeated problems in tackling the different question types.

Focus test 1 — Place value

Tenths, hundredths and thousandths follow a decimal point, which is used to separate whole numbers from decimals.

Read these and write each number in figures.

1 seventy-eight thousand one hundred and three _____

2 six hundred thousand four hundred and eighty _____

3 Write the number that is 100 more than each of these.

19 909 → _____   93 990 → _____   60 901 → _____

4 What is £345.75 rounded to the nearest pound? _____

5 Write the numbers at each arrow.

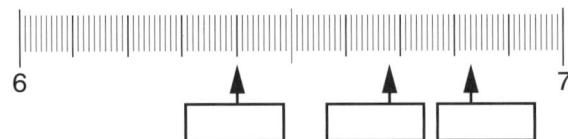

6 Complete these calculations.

17.02 × 100 = _____   27.4 × 100 = _____

7 Complete these calculations.

3005 ÷ 100 = _____   19 ÷ 100 = _____

8 Write these in order.   4.731   7.413   7.137   4.334

_____ < _____ < _____ < _____

9 Round each amount to the nearest whole number.

245.6 m → _____   853.91 ml → _____

10 Round each amount to the nearest tenth.

67.072 km → _____   391.745 kg → _____

11 Circle the smallest number and underline the largest number.

38.09   38.9   38.99   38.099   38.909

12 Mount Snowdon in Wales is 3560 feet in height. What is this rounded to the nearest 1000 feet? _____

Focus test 2 — Addition and subtraction

1. Join pairs of numbers that total 6.5.

   2.9   1.6   5.8   2.6   4.9
         0.7   3.9   3.6

> Decide whether to work out the answer in your head, use rough notes or use a written method – and always check that your answer makes sense.

Write the missing numbers to complete these.

2. ☐ 7 . 2 ☐
   + 4 ☐ . 4 7
   ‾‾‾‾‾‾‾‾‾‾‾
     8 6 . 7 2

3.   2 8 . ☐ 6
   − 1 ☐ . 6 ☐
   ‾‾‾‾‾‾‾‾‾‾‾
     1 0 . 7 7

4. Write the total weight of this group of parcels. _____   [9.45 kg] [12.6 kg] [13.07 kg]

5. A greenhouse costs £645.79. It costs an extra £87.54 to have it delivered and put up. What is the total cost? £ _____

6. Circle the two numbers with a difference of 2.7 and a total of 14.3.

   9.3   8.7   3.9   8.5   7.6   5.8

Complete these calculations.

7.   8 3 6 9 7
    + 4 1 6 7 2
    ‾‾‾‾‾‾‾‾‾‾‾

8.   5 0 0 6 8
    − 3 4 7 7 9
    ‾‾‾‾‾‾‾‾‾‾‾

9. What is the missing number? (17 − 8) + ____ = 14

10. Write in the missing digits 1, 2, 3, 4, 5 and 6.

    __.9 + 3.__ = 10.3   5.__ + __.9 = 7.1   __.6 + __.7 = 9.3

11. These are the bills for three meals at a café. What is the cost of each item?

    1 sandwich = _____   1 drink = _____
    1 ice cream = _____

    | 1 sandwich, 1 drink — Total: £3.70 |
    | 1 drink, 2 ice creams — Total: £3.10 |
    | 2 ice creams — Total: £1.80 |

12. What are the numbers A and B?

    A = ____   B = ____

    > A and B are two different whole numbers. A is 10 greater than B. A + B = 92

Now go to the Progress Chart to record your score!   Total ⬚   12

Focus test 3: Multiplication and division

1 Complete this multiplication grid.

×	9		8
7		21	
		54	

Remember: multiplication and division are inverse operations. Use this to help recall facts, for example:

3 × 6 = 18 and 6 × 3 = 18, so 18 ÷ 6 = 3 and 18 ÷ 3 = 6

2 Write the missing number.   7 × 8 × _____ = 560

3 Complete this calculation.   4 What is 2859 divided by 14?

```
   86
 × 95
 ____
```

14)2859 r____

5 A ball of string is 48 m in length. What length of string will there be in 20 balls? _____

6 This is a 'divide by 40' machine. Write the missing numbers in the chart.

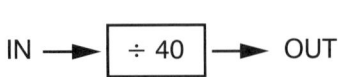

IN	160	___	440	___	360
OUT	___	5	___	20	___

7 Plums are sold in boxes of 12. How many complete boxes can be filled from a bag of 80 plums? _____

8 Fence panels are 1.5 m wide. The perimeter of a garden is 45 m. How many panels are needed to put a fence around the garden? _____

9 Which number between 80 and 90 has a remainder of 5 when it is divided by 9? _____

10 Complete this.

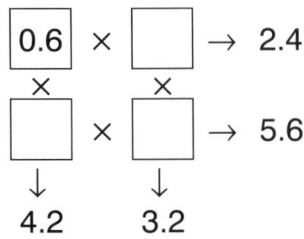

11 Complete these, writing in the correct signs: =, < or >.

17 × 8 _____ 16 × 9
135 ÷ 5 _____ 132 ÷ 4

12 Which number, when multiplied by 30, gives the same answer as 45 × 12? _____

Total 12

Focus test 4: Multiples, factors and prime numbers

1. Circle the numbers that are multiples of 6.

   72   92   114   87   69   99   106   80   96

2. Use each of these digits once to make a total that is a multiple of 5.

   [2] [9] [7] [6]   ☐☐ + ☐☐

3. 20 is a common multiple of 4 and 5. Which of these numbers is also a common multiple of 4 and 5? Circle the correct answer.

   9   16   60   30   45

4. What is the smallest number that is a common multiple of 4 and 6? _____

5. Circle the numbers that are **not** factors of 60.

   1   2   3   4   5   6   7   8   9

6. Write the missing factors for 72.

   (1, ___) (2, ___) (3, ___) (4, ___) (6, ___) (8, ___)

7. Write the factors of 36 in order, starting with 1.

   36 → 1 ___ ___ ___ ___ ___ ___ ___ ___

8. Write these numbers in the correct part of the Venn diagram.

   9   15   6   12   2
   10   20   36

   (Venn diagram: Multiple of 3 / Factor of 18)

9. What is the next prime number after the number 7? _____

Choose **two** of these digit cards each time to make 2-digit numbers.

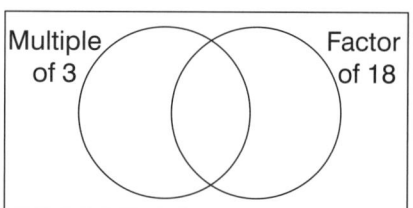

10. A factor of 60 → __ __

11. A multiple of 9 → __ __

12. A prime number → __ __

> A prime number only has two factors, 1 and itself. For example, 13 is a prime number as it can only be divided exactly by 1 and 13.

Now go to the Progress Chart to record your score!   Total   12

Focus test 5: Fractions, decimals and percentages

1. Answer these.

    $\frac{4}{5} + \frac{7}{10} = \square\frac{\square}{\square}$ $\frac{1}{2} - \frac{1}{3} = \frac{\square}{\square}$

2. Write the missing percentage or decimal to complete this table.

0.3	___	0.95	___	0.08
30%	70%	___	5%	___

3. Circle the fraction that is the same as the decimal number.

    0.2 $\frac{1}{5}$ $\frac{1}{4}$ $\frac{1}{2}$ $\frac{3}{4}$

4. Join each improper fraction to the mixed number with the same value.

    $\frac{7}{3}$ $\frac{7}{5}$ $\frac{13}{5}$ $\frac{5}{3}$

    $1\frac{2}{5}$ $2\frac{3}{5}$ $1\frac{2}{3}$ $2\frac{1}{3}$

5. What is $\frac{3}{8}$ of 48? _____

6. Write <, > or = between each pair of fractions.

    $\frac{2}{5}$ ___ $\frac{1}{4}$ $\frac{1}{2}$ ___ $\frac{7}{10}$ $\frac{3}{4}$ ___ $\frac{2}{3}$

Write the following fractions as percentages.

7. $\frac{7}{10}$ = _____   8. $\frac{2}{5}$ = _____   9. $\frac{3}{4}$ = _____

> To change fractions to percentages find an equivalent fraction with the denominator 100.
> $\frac{3}{5}$ is equivalent to $\frac{60}{100}$
> $\frac{3}{5}$ = 60%

10. Change these test scores to percentages.

    8 out of 10 → _____%

    16 out of 20 → _____%

    8 out of 25 → _____%

11. Circle the two cards that show less than $\frac{1}{2}$

    $\frac{5}{7}$ 5%   .52   0.7   52%

12. Look at this circle.

    What percentage of this circle is shaded? _____

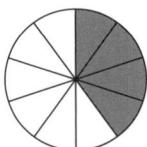

Now go to the Progress Chart to record your score!   Total   12

Focus test 6 — Number sequences

> You can often find the pattern or rule in a sequence by looking at the difference between the numbers.

1. What is the next number in this sequence?

    137   133   129   125   ____

2. What is the missing number in this sequence? Circle the correct answer.

    121   100   ____   64   49   36   25

    a 85   b 76   c 81   d 90

Write the missing numbers in these sequences.

3. ____   179   190   201   ____   223

4. 6.5   ____   ____   11   12.5   14

5. 6540   6450   ____   6270   6180   ____

6. In this sequence each number is half the previous number.

    ____   ____   176   88   44   ____   ____

7. In this sequence each number is double the previous number.

    ____   ____   18   36   72   ____   ____

8. What is the rule or pattern for this sequence? Circle the correct answer.

    | 8279 8079 7879 7679 | a – 20   b – 200   c – 2000   d – 2

9. What is the next number in this sequence?

    64   81   100   ____

10. Write the next number in this sequence.

    1   3   6   10   ____

11. Describe the rule or pattern in the sequence above.
    _____

12. Write the missing numbers in this sequence.

    630   ____   642   ____   654

Now go to the Progress Chart to record your score!   Total   12

Focus test 7 — Shapes and angles

Look at these shapes.

1 Which two shapes have no right angles? Shapes ____ and ____

2 What is the name of shape E? _____

3 Which shape has no lines of symmetry? ____

4 Which shape is not a quadrilateral? ____

5 Tick to show whether each angle is acute, obtuse, reflex or right-angled.

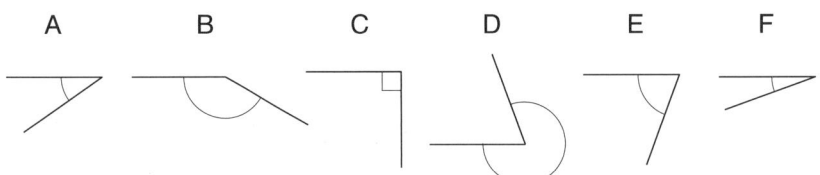

Angle	A	B	C	D	E	F
Acute						
Obtuse						
Reflex						
Right-angled						

6 Count the edges, faces and vertices on each shape and complete the chart.

Shape	Name	Faces	Edges	Vertices
	Square-based pyramid	____	____	____
	Tetrahedron	____	____	____
	Cuboid	____	____	____
	Triangular prism	____	____	____

> The net of a solid or 3-D shape is what it looks like when it is opened out flat.

Name each of these shapes from the nets.

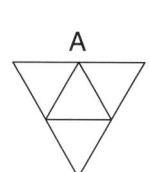 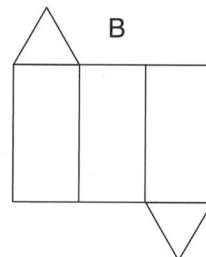 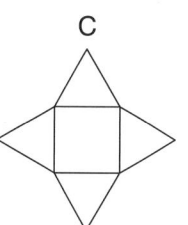

7 A _____

8 B _____

9 C _____

10 Draw a reflection of this shape. Use a ruler.

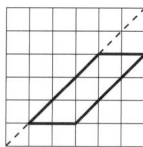

11 Measure angle A accurately. Use a protractor.

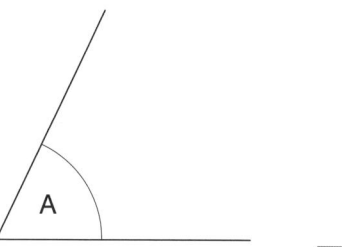

_____°

12 Write the size of the missing angle for each shape. Do not use a protractor.

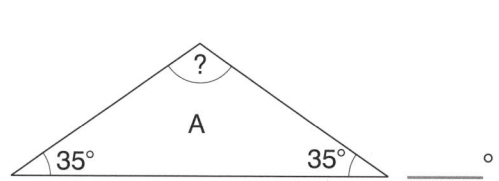 _____°

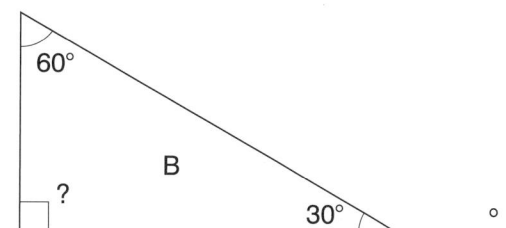 _____°

Now go to the Progress Chart to record your score!   Total   12

Focus test 8 — Area and perimeter

Note: 'Not drawn to scale'

Area is usually measured in square centimetres or square metres, written as cm² and m². Always remember to write this at the end of the measurement.

Calculate the area and perimeter of these rectangles.

1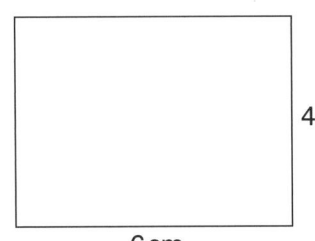
4.5 cm
6 cm

Area = _____

Perimeter = _____

2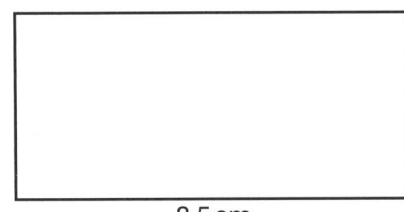
4 cm
8.5 cm

Area = _____

Perimeter = _____

3 What is the perimeter of a square swimming pool with an area of 48 m²? _____

Calculate the area of the shapes on this 1 cm square grid.

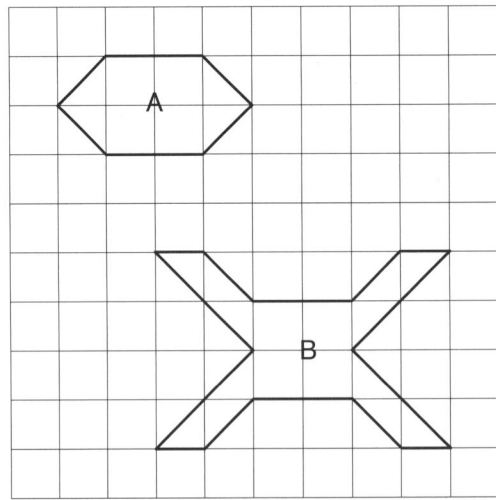

4 Shape A = ____ cm²

5 Shape B = ____ cm²

6 What is the area of a square tile with a 20 cm side? _____

7 The area of a rectangle is 36 cm². One of the sides is 4 cm. What is the perimeter of the rectangle? _____

8 The perimeter of a rectangle is 24 cm. The length is double the width. What is the area of this rectangle?

Area = _____ cm²

Calculate the area of these shaded shapes.

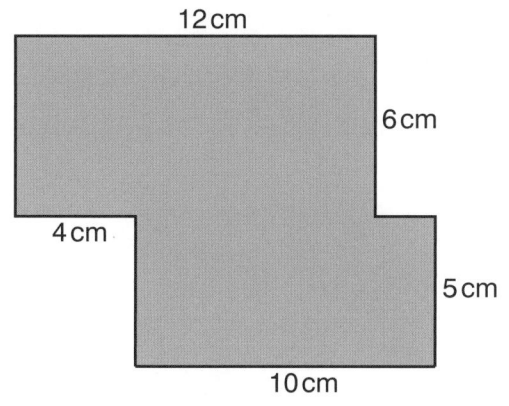

9 Area = _____ cm²

10 Area = _____ cm²

11 Which has the larger area? Underline the statement that is true.

    A has the larger area   B has the larger area

    The areas of A and B are the same.

12 Which has the longer perimeter, Shape A or Shape B? _____

Now go to the Progress Chart to record your score!   Total   12

Focus test 9 — Measures

1 What is the difference between the amount of liquid in these two jugs?

_____

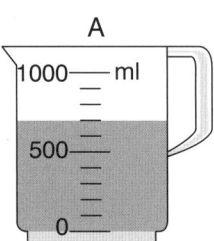 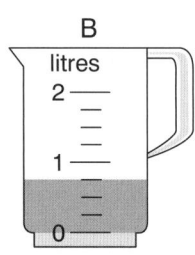

Read scales carefully when measuring – look at the numbers written on the scales and work out the value of each unnumbered mark.

2 The liquid in these two jugs is poured into an empty bottle. How much liquid is in the bottle? _____

3 Write this set of measures in length order, starting with the smallest.

   7.6 cm   70 mm   7.2 m   78 cm   0.75 m

_____ _____ _____ _____ _____

Smallest →

4 Sam is baking some cakes. He puts some flour on the scales and then adds some butter.

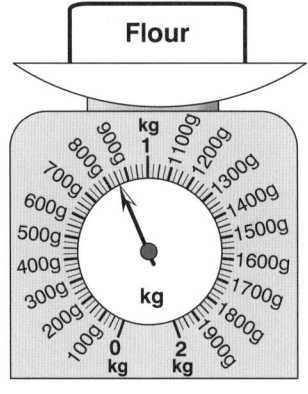 

The weight of the flour is _____ g.

The weight of the butter is _____ g.

The total weight of the flour and butter is _____ kg _____ g.

5 A bus should arrive at 10:55 am but it is 12 minutes late. What time does the bus arrive?

_____

6 Write the missing times on this train timetable. Each train starts in Arden and takes the same amount of time to travel between each station.

Arden	09:50	11:28	____
Blythe	____	11:46	13:25
Chorton	10:34	____	13:51
Dunley	10:52	____	____

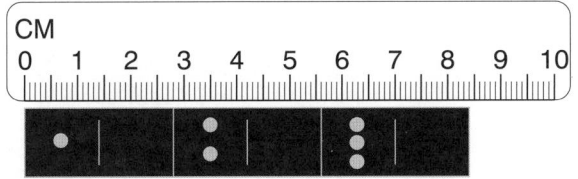

7 What is the total length of three dominoes? ____ cm

8 What is the total length of five dominoes? ____ cm

9 What is the difference in temperature between this pair of thermometers?

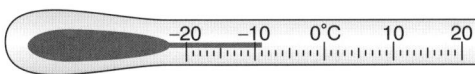 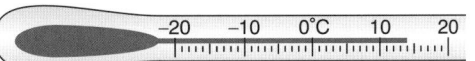

____ °C

10 Each of these boxes is a different weight.

Boxes A and B weigh 14 kg altogether.

Box C weighs 4 kg more than Box A.

Boxes A and C weigh 16 kg altogether.

What is the weight of each box?

Box A ____

Box B ____

Box C ____

11 Calculate this division. Give your answer in the unit of measurement shown.

1.56 litres ÷ 6 = ____ ml

12 Write < or > to make this sentence true.

63 mm ____ 3.6 cm ____ 3.06 m ____ 360 cm ____ 36 mm

Focus test 10 — Transformations and coordinates

These show three types of transformation of shape A:

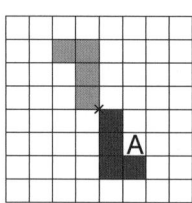
Rotation

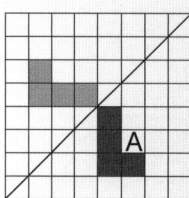
Reflection

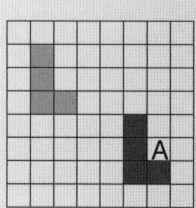
Translation

Write the correct transformation – **rotation**, **reflection** or **translation** – for each of these.

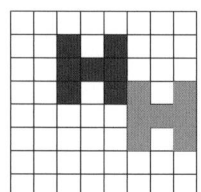
1 _____

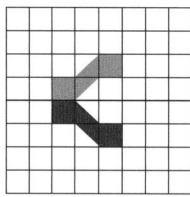
2 _____

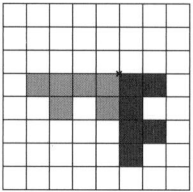
3 _____

4 Reflect the first tile in the tile next to it and below it. Continue the pattern to complete the whole grid.

(4, 1), (4, 6) and (0, 1) are the three vertices of a right-angled triangle.

5 (4,1) is already marked on this grid. Plot the other two points and draw the triangle.

6 Circle the coordinates that are enclosed by the sides of the triangle.

(2, 2)   (3, 3)   (2, 4)

(1, 3)   (2, 3)   (3, 4)

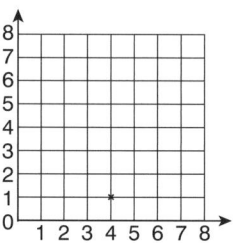

7 A, B and C are three vertices of a parallelogram. What are the coordinates of the fourth vertex, D? _____

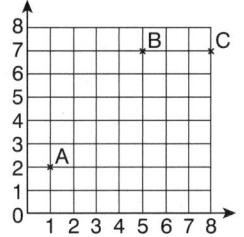

8 The parallelogram is translated to a new position on the grid. Vertex A is moved from (1, 2) to (0, 0). What are the new coordinates of the other three vertices?

B → _____   C → _____   D → _____

9 What are the missing coordinates for this square? (____, ____)

(11,17)   (16,17)

(?, ?)   (16,12)

10 Mark coordinate (−4, 2) on the grid. This is the fourth vertex of a quadrilateral. Draw two lines to complete this shape.

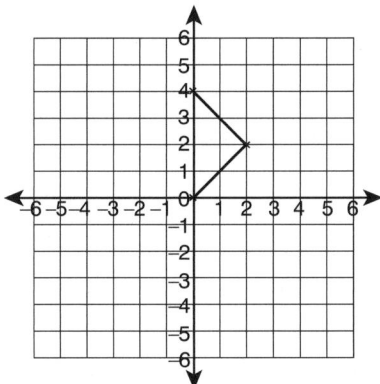

11 Coordinates (−1, 2) and (1, 2) are both on the line of symmetry of this shape.

True or False? _____

12 The shape is rotated anticlockwise around point (2, 2) so that the vertex at (−4, 2) is now at (2, −4). Where is the new position of the vertex at (0, 0)? _____

Now go to the Progress Chart to record your score!   Total   12

Focus test 11 — Charts, graphs and tables

This chart shows the height and shoe size for each child in a class.

1. How many children are taller than 149 cm? _____

2. How many children wear a shoe smaller than size 5? _____

3. How many children wear size 4 shoes and are shorter than 140 cm? _____

4. How many children are taller than 129 cm and wear a shoe size more than 4? _____

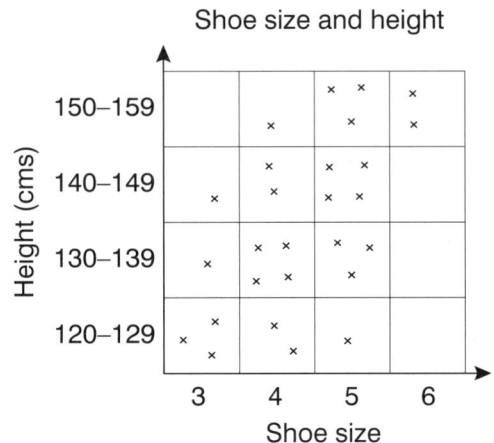

This graph shows the time and distance of a bus route.

A distance–time line graph like this is continuous, so every point on the line has a value.

5. How many minutes in total is the bus at bus stops during the journey? _____

6. How many miles does the bus travel between 3:30 and 3:45? _____

7. How many miles in total does the bus travel? _____

8 This timetable shows the times the bus leaves each bus stop.

Use the graph to complete the two missing times.

Name of bus stop	Time bus departs
Anton	3:00pm
Bodham	3:15pm
Canby	_____pm
Duffield	3:45pm
Edgemore	4:00pm
Fenwell	4:10pm
Greatley	4:30pm
Heathend	_____pm
Town centre arrival time	5:05pm

In a science lesson a class measured the length of a shadow every 30 minutes and recorded the results on this graph.

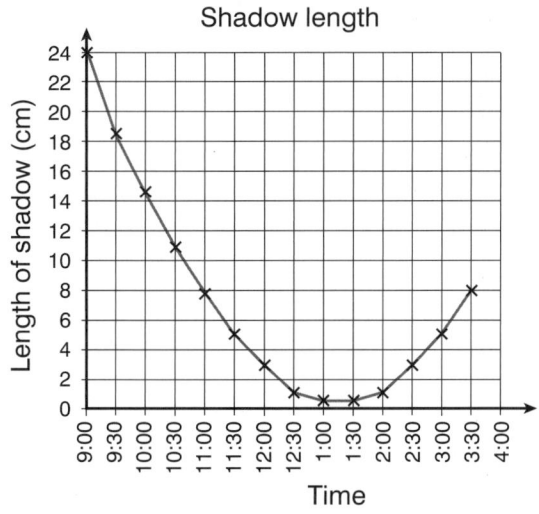

9 What length was the shadow at its shortest? _____

10 At approximately what time was the shadow 21 cm in length? _____

11 Circle the time period in which the shadow length decreased most quickly.

        9:00–9:30   9:30–10:00   10:00–10:30

12 By how many centimetres did the shadow increase in length between 2 o'clock and 3 o'clock? _____

Focus test 12: Mean, median, mode and probability

> Remember: to find the mean add together all the scores and then divide that total by the number of scores you have used. The mean of 3, 5, 7 and 9 is 6.
>
> 3 + 5 + 7 + 9 = 24, divided by 4 is 6.

Look at this set of numbers.

(13) (29) (18) (21) (29)

1 The mean is _____

2 The median is _____

3 The mode is _____

4 The mean of six numbers is 3.5. The lowest number is 2, the range is 5 and the modes are 2 and 3, with two of each of these numbers.

What are the six numbers? _____ _____ _____ _____ _____ _____

Look at the group of coins.

5 What coin value is the mode? _____

6 What is the mean value of the coins? _____

7 Which coin value is the median? _____

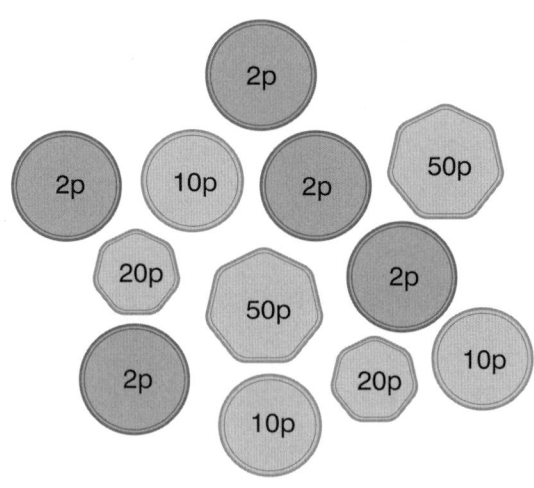

These are the weights of six parcels.

8 What is the mean weight? _____

9 What is the mode? _____

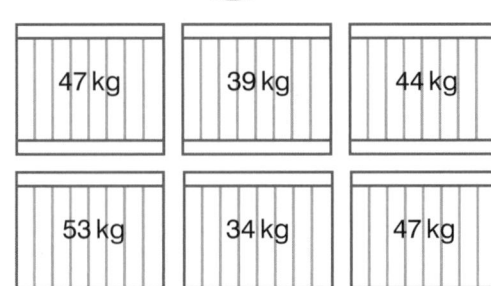

10 Write colours on this spinner so that you are equally likely to spin the colour blue as you are to spin green.

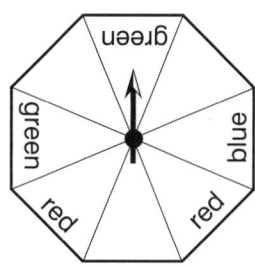

11 Spinner A has the numbers 1–5 and Spinner B has the numbers 1–6.

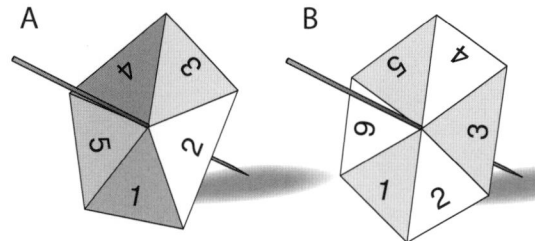

Circle the chance of spinning an odd number on Spinner A.

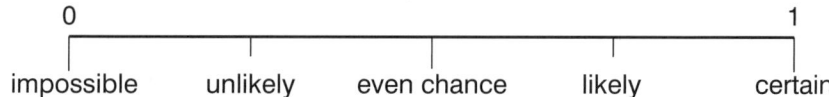

Circle the chance of spinning a 6 on Spinner A.

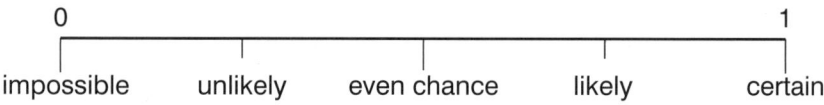

Circle the chance of spinning an odd number on Spinner B.

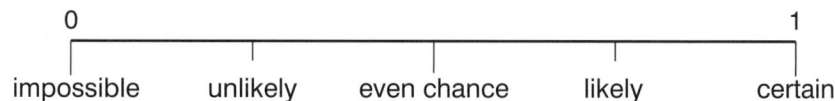

Circle the chance of spinning a multiple of 3 on Spinner B.

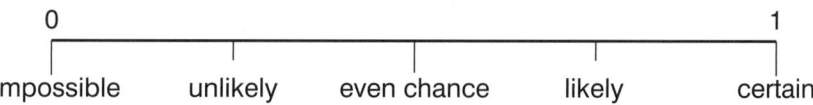

12 What is the likelihood of rolling a 7 on a 1–6 dice?

impossible   poor chance   even chance

good chance   certain

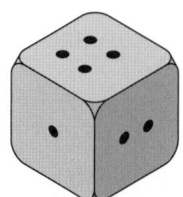

Mixed paper 1

Circle the digit in each number that represents the number written in words.

1. 222 222 two thousand
2. 666 666 six hundred thousand
3. 111 111 one hundred
4. 444 444 forty thousand

5–8 Write the missing numbers on this addition grid.

+	0.365	1.74
12.6		
	4.97	

Complete these, writing in the correct signs: =, < or >.

9. 7 × 4 ____ 3 × 9
10. 6 × 6 ____ 9 × 4
11. 49 ÷ 7 ____ 48 ÷ 6
12. 56 ÷ 8 ____ 54 ÷ 9
13. Divide 45.5 by 0.35. ____

Use these numbers to answer each question. 25 26 27 28 29

14. Which number is a multiple of 3? ____
15. Which number is a common multiple of both 2 and 7? ____
16. Which number is a prime number? ____
17. Which number is a factor of 84? ____

Answer these.

18. $2\frac{13}{20} - 1\frac{14}{15} = \boxed{\frac{\Box}{\Box}}$
19. 72% of 300 + $\frac{5}{6}$ of 84 = ____

Write these decimals as percentages.

20. 0.7 = ____ %
21. 0.15 = ____ %

Write the next number in each sequence.

22. 0.2   1.7   3.2   4.7   ____
23. 81   64   49   36   ____

Write the missing numbers in these sequences.

24 −12.9   −9.3   −5.7   −2.1   _____

25 15   30   60   _____   240   480   960

26–29 Complete the chart.

Shape name	Number of vertices	Number of edges
Pentagonal-based pyramid	_____	_____
Hexagonal prism	_____	_____

Four identical rectangles form the shape below.

30 Calculate the area of the white shape in the centre. _____ cm²

31 Calculate the total area of the grey, shaded sections. _____ cm²

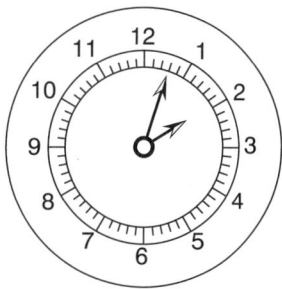
5 cm
8 cm

32 A square table has an area of 4 m². What is the length of one side of this table? _____ m

33 A shop wants to put flashing lights all the way round a window. The window is 120 cm wide by 325 cm high. Circle the length of lights that is the exact length to go the whole way round the window.

  a 890 cm   **b** 900 cm   **c** 880 cm   **d** 980 cm

34 A cake is put in the oven at this time and needs to cook for 15 minutes. What time is the cake ready to take out of the oven? _____

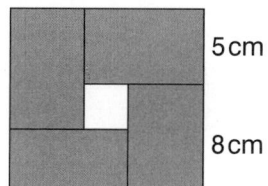

35 What is the difference between these two temperatures? _____ °C

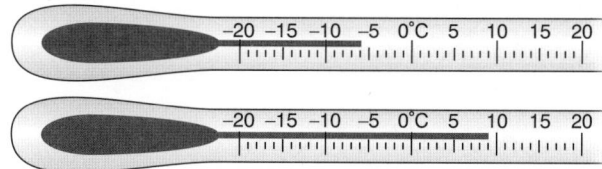

Write <, > or = to make each statement true.

36 33.3 km _____ 3330 m   **37** 60 ml _____ 0.06 litres

Write the word that describes the transformation of the triangle in each question. Choose from **rotation**, **reflection** or **translation**.

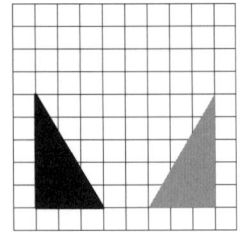

38 _____

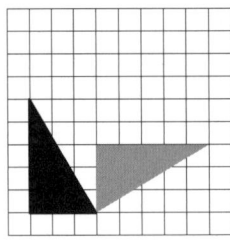

39 _____

40 _____

41 Coordinates (1, 0), (2, 3) and (6, 3) are all on this line. True or False?

_____

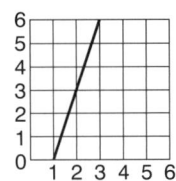

These are the distances and times of a cyclist in the London to Brighton cycle race.

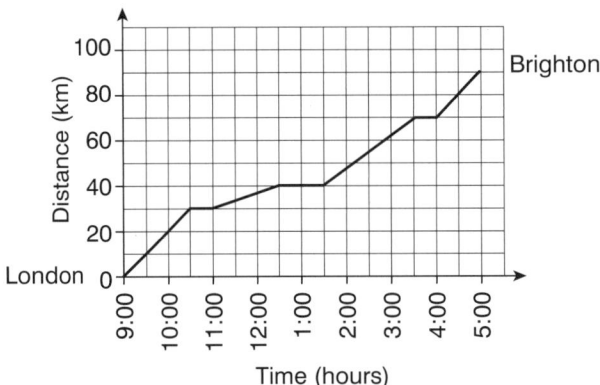

42 How far had the cyclist travelled by 10:30? _____

43 What was the time when the cyclist had cycled 55 km? _____

44 How long did the cyclist stop to rest altogether? _____

45 How far did the cyclist travel in total? _____

These are the heights of seven children.

Lee 157 cm   Sam 152 cm   Jo 148 cm   Ben 145 cm
Eve 152 cm   Kay 150 cm   Nicky 149 cm

46 Which is the median height? _____

47 Which height is the mode? _____

48 What is the mean height, rounded to the nearest whole centimetre? _____

Choose one of these words to answer the questions.

> impossible   poor chance   even chance
> good chance   certain

49 What is the chance of throwing a 6 on a dice? _____

50 What is the chance of throwing a number less than 7 on a dice? _____

Now go to the Progress Chart to record your score!   Total 50

Mixed paper 2

Write the number that is 100 more than each of these.

1 77 945 → _____   2 50 982 → _____

3 16 900 → _____   4 38 199 → _____

5 What is fifty-seven thousand, two hundred and sixty-nine plus forty-eight thousand, nine hundred and six? _____

6 What number is eighteen thousand, eight hundred and eighty-eight less than twenty-three thousand, three hundred and twenty-three?

7 Write these numbers in order, starting with the smallest.

   1.2   1.001   1.011   1.101   10.01

   _____ _____ _____ _____ _____

   Smallest →

8 How much change is there from £20 if Lily buys 3 sandwiches at £3.26 each, plus 3 drinks at £1.80 each and 3 bags of fruit at 79p each? ____

9 Look at these number cards:

   5 9 1 6 2 8 3

Place one number in each position to find the smallest number that is divisible by 5. Each number can be used once only.

___ ___ ___ ___ ___ ___ ___

10 What number when divided by 12 has an answer of 4 remainder 5?
_____

11 Which number, when multiplied by 40, gives the same answer as 8 × 30? _____

Underline the correct answer.

12 0.3 × 9 =   0.027   0.27   2.7   2.07   27

13 0.84 × 0.3 =   0.025   0.252   3.4   2.52   3.24

14–19 Write these numbers in the correct part of the Venn diagram.

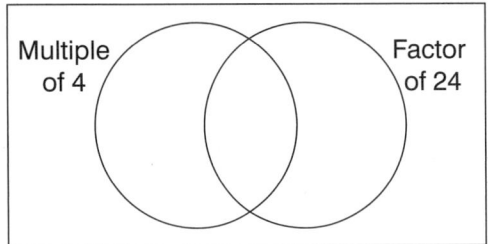
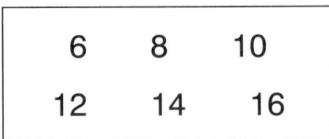

Circle the fraction that is the same as the decimal number.

20 0.8 $\frac{1}{8}$ $\frac{3}{4}$ $\frac{4}{5}$ $\frac{2}{3}$ $\frac{5}{8}$

21 6.75 $6\frac{5}{7}$ $3\frac{1}{4}$ $7\frac{5}{6}$ $6\frac{3}{4}$ $6\frac{4}{5}$

Write <, > or = between each pair of fractions.

22 $\frac{2}{5}$ ____ $\frac{5}{15}$ 23 $\frac{3}{4}$ ____ $\frac{9}{12}$

24 The rule for this sequence is to add the last two numbers together, then multiply the answer by 2. What is the next number in this sequence?

   4   6   20   52   144   ____

25 The rule for this sequence is to multiply the last two numbers together, then halve the answer. What is the next number in this sequence?

   2   4   4   8   16   ____

Write the next number in these sequences.

26 −24.3   −19.6   −14.9   −10.2   ____

27 12.21   8.67   5.13   1.59   ____

Write the name of the shape described in each question. Choose from this list:

    Rectangle   Tetrahedron   Cylinder   Regular hexagon

    Sphere   Rhombus   Triangular prism

28 Name the flat shape that has 6 equal length sides and 6 lines of symmetry. ____

29 Name the 2-D shape that has 4 right angles, 2 pairs of different length sides and 2 lines of symmetry. ____

30 Name the solid shape that has 4 triangular faces, 6 edges and 4 vertices. ____

31 Name the 3-D shape that has no vertices, 2 edges and 2 circular faces.

____

32–33 A classroom is 7.5 m wide and 10 m long. Calculate the area and perimeter of this classroom.

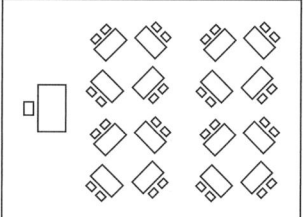

Area = ____ m²

Perimeter = ____ m

The area of a rectangle is 32 cm. It is twice as long as it is wide.

34 What is the length of this rectangle? ____ cm

35 What is the width of this rectangle? ____ cm

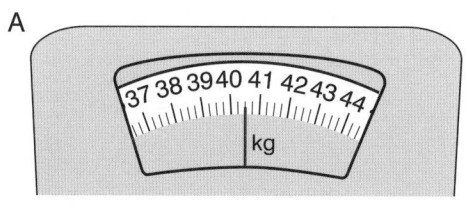
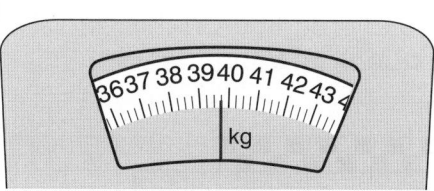

36 Which scale shows the heavier weight, A or B? ____

37 What is the total weight of these two amounts? ____ kg

38 What is the total in kilograms of these weights?

120 g + 1250 g + 0.75 kg + 3.2 kg + 12.57 kg = ____

39 Look at the first flag. Circle the flag that is a **rotation** of the first flag.

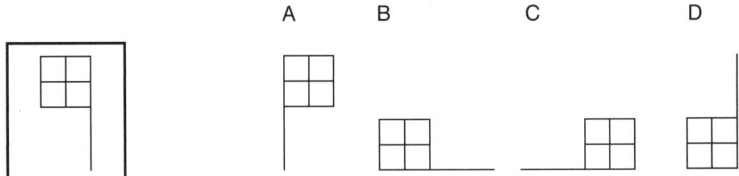

40 Look at the first triangle. Circle the triangle that is a **reflection** of the first triangle.

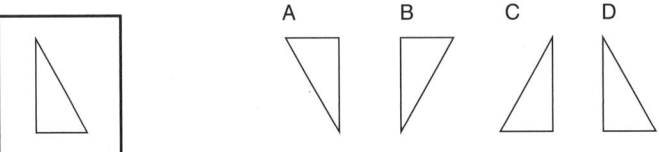

41 Write the coordinates for A.
(____, ____)

42 Mark coordinate (–4, 3) on the grid and label it B.

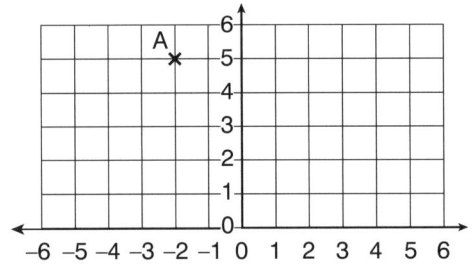

This chart shows the clothes sold in a shop in January.

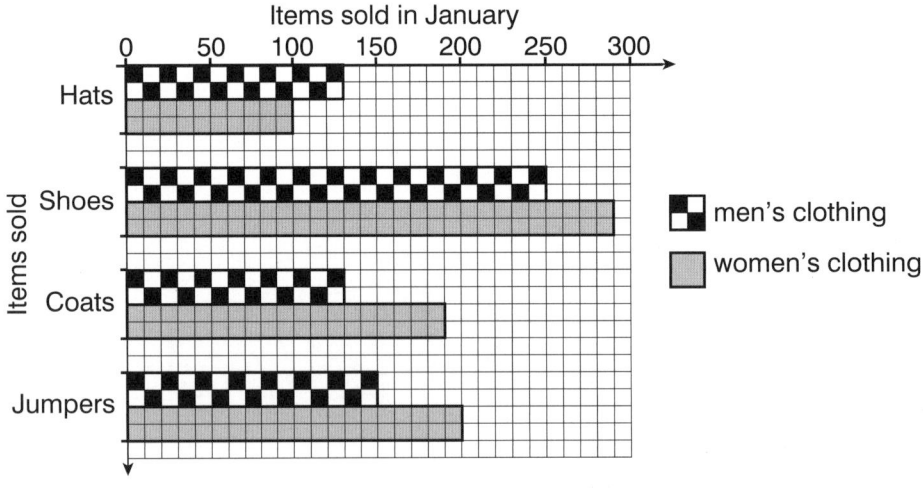

43 How many men's coats were sold? _____

44 How many more women's shoes were sold than men's shoes? _____

Any answer that requires units of measurement should be marked wrong if the correct units have not been included.

Focus Test 1: Place value (page 4)

1. **78 103**
2. **600 480**
3. **20 009, 94 090, 61 001** To add 100, place the numbers on a decimal grid. To make a number larger, find the hundreds column and make the number one larger. When the number in the hundreds column is already a 9, adding 1 makes the number 10, so put a 0 in the hundreds column and add one in the thousands column. In the first example, the thousands column also has a 9 in it. Adding 1 makes the number 10, so put a 0 in the thousands column and add one in the ten-thousands column.

TTh	Th	H	T	U
1	9	9	0	9
+		1	0	0
2	0	0	0	9
1	1			

TTh	Th	H	T	U
9	3	9	9	0
+		1	0	0
9	4	0	9	0
	1			

TTh	Th	H	T	U
6	0	9	0	1
+		1	0	0
6	1	0	0	1
	1			

4. **£346** When rounding a number to the nearest pound, look at the number in the tenths column. If it is 4 or below, leave the number in the ones column unchanged. If it is 5 or above, raise the number in the ones column by 1.

Th	H	T	U	•	t	h	th
	3	4	5	•	7	5	
	3	4	6				

5. **6.4, 6.68, 6.83** There are 10 increments between 6 and 7, and each increment has been divided into 10. Work out the increment between 6 and 7 first to provide the number in the tenths column. Then work out the smaller increment to find the number in the hundredths column.

6. **1702, 2740** To multiply by 100, place the numbers on a decimal grid. To make a number larger by 100 times, move the numbers to the left twice. If there is nothing in the ones column, place a 0 in it.

Th	H	T	U	•	t	h	th
		1	7	•	0	2	
1	7	0	2				
			2	7	•	4	
2	7	4	0				

7. **30.05, 0.19** To divide by 100, place the numbers on a decimal grid. To make a number 100 times smaller, move the numbers to the right twice. If there is nothing in the ones column, place a 0 in it.

Th	H	T	U	•	t	h	th
3	0	0	5				
		3	0	•	0	5	
			1	9			
			0	•	1	9	

8. **4.334 < 4.731 < 7.137 < 7.413** To order numbers from smallest to largest, write them in a column so that the decimal points line up or place them on a decimal grid. Begin with the smallest numbers on the far left and work towards the right. As 4 is the same number, look at 4.7 and 4.3, putting the smallest number first.

9. **246 m, 854 ml** When rounding a number to the nearest one, look at the number in the tenths column. If it is 4 or below, leave the number in the ones column unchanged. If it is 5 or above, raise the number in the ones column by 1.

10. **67.1 km, 391.7 kg** When rounding a number to the nearest tenth, look at the number in the hundredths column. If it is 4 or below, leave the number in the tenths column unchanged. If it is 5 or above, raise the number in the tenths column by 1.

11. **(38.09), 38.99** To order numbers from smallest to largest, place them in a decimal grid. Begin with the smallest numbers on the far left and work towards the right. As all of these numbers begin with 38, look at numbers in the tenths column and then the hundredths column.

T	U	•	t	h	th
3	8	•	0	9	
3	8	•	9		
3	8	•	9	9	
3	8	•	0	9	9
3	8	•	9	0	9

12 **4000 feet** When rounding a number to the nearest 1000, look at the number in the hundreds column. If it is 4 or below, leave the number in the thousands column unchanged. If it is 5 or above, raise the number in the thousands column by 1.

Focus Test 2: Addition and subtraction (page 5)

1 **(2.9, 3.6) (1.6, 4.9) (5.8, 0.7) (2.6, 3.9)** Look for numbers in the tenths column that when added together, make 5.

2–3 Use logic to work out the missing digits, then solve the equation to check if the answer works.

2   37.25
  + 49.47
    86.72

Find the 5 by working out what number needs to be added to 7 to make a number ending in 2. 5 + 7 = 12 and the 1 is carried over. Find the 9 by working out what number needs to be added to 7 to make a number ending in 6. 7 + 9 = 16 and the 1 is carried over. Find the 3 by working out what number needs to be added to 4 and the carried over 1 to make 8. 3 + 4 + 1 = 8

3   28.**4**6
   –17.**6**9
    10.77

Find the 9 by subtracting the 7 from a number ending in 6. 16 – 9 = 7 and the 1 is borrowed from the 4. Find the 4 by adding the 6 to the 7 and the borrowed 1. 6 + 7 + 1 = 14 and the 1 is borrowed from the 8. Find the 7 by subtracting the 1 from the 8 to make 7 and this is subtracted to make 0.

4–5 To add up amounts with a different number of digits, write out the numbers in a column with the decimal point in the same place and adding a 0 for missing values.

4 **35.12 kg**
    09.45
    12.60
  + 13.07
    35.12

5 **£733.33**
    £645.79
  + £87.54
    £733.33

6 9.3   8.7   3.9 (**8.5**) 7.6 (**5.8**) Look for two numbers where the tenths add up to 3 (remember that they might add up to 13 instead). The two numbers could be 8.7 + 7.6, but 8 + 7 makes too large a total. Another pair where the tenths add up to 13 is 8.5 + 5.8.

7 **125 369** Use column addition (See Focus test 1, Q3) to solve the sum.

8 **15 289** Use column subtraction (See Focus test 1, Q3) to solve this calculation.

9 **5** (17 – 8) + 5 = 14; 17 – 8 = 9 then 14 – 9 = 5

10 **6.**9 + 3.**4**, 5.**2** + 1.9, 3.6 + **5.7** *or* **5.**6 + **3.**7 To find the 6 and 4, subtract 3.9 from 10.3. To find the 2 and 1, subtract 5.9 from 7.1. To find the 3 and 5, subtract 1.3 from 9.3 and place the 3 and 5 in either order.

11 **1 sandwich = £2.40, 1 drink = £1.30, 1 ice cream = 90p** Find the cost of one ice cream first by dividing £1.80 by 2 to find 90p. Next find the cost of one drink by subtracting 2 ice creams from £3.10 to find £1.30. Finally, find the cost of one sandwich by subtracting the cost of one drink from £3.70 to find £2.40.

12 **51, 41** To find this, divide 92 by 2 to make both A and B equal: 92 ÷ 2 = 46. To make a difference of 10 between the numbers, divide 10 by 2 to make 5, then add 5 to one number and subtract 5 from the other number: 46 + 5 = 51; 46 – 5 = 41.

Focus Test 3: Multiplication and division (page 6)

1

×	9	3	8
7	63	21	56
6	54	18	48

The second column has a 9 in it and the first row has a 7 in it, so the first space is 9 × 7 = 63. The other number in the first column is 54, so the third row heading must be 6 as 54 ÷ 9 = 6. The third column heading must be a 3 as 21 ÷ 7 = 3. The number 3 multiplied by the row heading 6 is 18. In the last column, the heading is 8. Multiplying that by the row heading 7 gives 56 and 8 × 6 = 48.

2 **10** 7 × 8 × 10 = 560; 7 × 8 = 56 then 56 × 10 = 560

3 **8170**
      86
   × 95
     430
    7740
    8170

4 **204 r3** Use 'bus stop' division to solve the calculation. 14 into 28 goes 2 times with a remainder of 0, so write 2 above the 28. 14 is too big to go into 5, so write 0 above the 5 and carry the 5 over to the next column to create the number 59. 14 into 59 goes 4 times with a remainder of 3, so write 4 above the 9 and add the remainder at the end.

```
      2 0 4 r 3
  1 4 ) 2 8 5 9
```

5 **960 m** Multiply 48 m by 2 to find 96 m and then multiply this by 10 to find 960 m.

6
IN	160	**200**	440	**800**	360
OUT	**4**	5	**11**	20	**9**

The function machine divides the top number by 40. To find the 'In' numbers, multiply the 'Out' numbers by 40.

7 **6** Divide 80 by 12 and round down as the boxes must be completely filled.

8 **30** Divide 45 m by 1.5. It is easier to divide whole numbers, so adding two fence panels together to make a multiple of 3 is easier. 45 ÷ 3 = 15 and 15 × 2 fence panels = 30.

9 **86** The only multiple in the 9 times table between 80 and 90 is 81. Add on the remainder of 5 to make 86.

10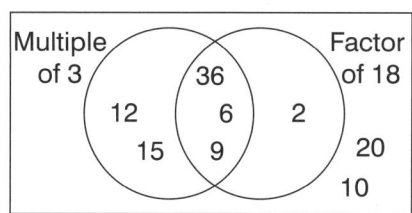

To find 4, divide 2.4 by 0.6. To find 7, divide 4.2 by 0.6. To find 0.8, divide 3.2 by 4. To divide a number with a decimal point, multiply both of them by 10 to make whole numbers: 42 ÷ 6 = 7, 24 ÷ 6 = 4, 56 ÷ 70 = 0.8.

11 **<, <** Find the answer to both sides first and then place the small point of the sign pointing to the smaller number. 17 × 8 = 136 < 16 × 9 = 144; 135 ÷ 5 = 27 < 132 ÷ 4 = 33

12 **18** 45 × 12 = 540 then 540 ÷ 30 = 18

Focus Test 4: Multiples, factors and prime numbers (page 7)

1 **72, 114, 96** To find the multiples of 6, divide each number by 6, making sure it fits in without any remainder.

2 **79 + 26** or **29 + 76** Every multiple of 5 must end in a 5 or a 0 and numbers ending in 9 and 6 would make a multiple of 5 when added together.

3 **60** Any multiple of 20 will also be a common multiple of 4 and 5.

4 **12** To find the smallest common multiple, place the first few multiples of both 4 and 6 in order until there is a number that appears in both sequences:
4, 8, **12**
6, **12**

5 **7, 8, 9** To find the factors of 60, list the pairs of numbers that fit exactly into 60: 1 × 60, 2 × 30, 4 × 15, 5 × 12, 6 × 10.

6 **72, 36, 24, 18, 12, 9** To find the factor pairs, divide 72 by the given numbers: 72 ÷ 1 = 72; 72 ÷ 2 = 36; 72 ÷ 3 = 24; 72 ÷ 4 = 18; 72 ÷ 6 = 12; 72 ÷ 8 = 9.

7 **2, 3, 4, 6, 9, 12, 18, 36** Find the factor pairs and then place the numbers in order.

8

Venn diagram: Multiple of 3 | Factor of 18
Left only: 12, 15
Intersection: 36, 6, 9
Right only: 2, 20
Outside: 10

First find the multiples of 3 and then the factors of 18. Find the common numbers and place them into the middle space shared by both circles. The space on the left has all the multiples of 3 that are not shared and the space on the right circle has all the factors of 18 that are not shared. The numbers 10 and 20 are neither multiples of 3 nor factors of 18 so they must go outside of the circles.

9 **11** A prime number is any number that can only be divided by itself or 1.

10 **1 and 5** The number 15 is a factor of 60 (15 × 4).

11 **4 and 5** The numbers 45 and 54 are both multiples of 9 (9 × 5, 9 × 6).

12 **7 and 1, 4 and 1,** or **4 and 7** The numbers 71, 17, 41 and 47 are all prime numbers.

Focus Test 5: Fractions, decimals and percentages (page 8)

1 $1\frac{1}{2}, \frac{1}{6}$ To add fractions together, or to subtract them, first find equivalent fractions so that the bottom numbers (the denominators) are the same. Remember to only add or subtract the numerators, not the denominators, and to put the answer in its simplest form.
$\frac{4}{5} = \frac{8}{10}; \frac{8}{10} + \frac{7}{10} = \frac{15}{10}; \frac{15}{10} = 1\frac{5}{10} = 1\frac{1}{2}$
$\frac{1}{2} = \frac{3}{6}$ and $\frac{1}{3} = \frac{2}{6}; \frac{3}{6} - \frac{2}{6} = \frac{1}{6}$

2
0.3	**0.7**	0.95	**0.05**	0.08
30%	70%	**95%**	5%	**8%**

To find a percentage from a decimal, place the decimal numbers into hundredths, then take the tenths and hundredths to form the percentage. 0.3 = 0.30 = 30%; 0.95 = 95%; 0.08 = 8%
To find a decimal from a percentage, place the tens and units digits after a decimal point. 70% = 0.70 = 0.7; 5% = 0.05

3 $\frac{1}{5}$ To convert a decimal to a fraction, place the decimal on a decimal grid and then create a fraction in tenths, hundredths or thousandths.

Then reduce the fraction to its simplest form.

T	U	.	t	h	th
	0	.	2		

$0.2 = \frac{2}{10} = \frac{1}{5}$

4 $\frac{7}{3} = 2\frac{1}{3}, \frac{7}{5} = 1\frac{2}{5}, \frac{13}{5} = 2\frac{3}{5}, \frac{5}{3} = 1\frac{2}{3}$ To turn an improper fraction to a mixed number, divide the denominator into the numerator and leave the remaining number as a fraction. For example, $\frac{7}{3}$ 7 ÷ 3 = 2 r 1 = $2\frac{1}{3}$

5 **18** To find a fraction of a number, divide the number by the denominator and then multiply the answer by the numerator. 48 ÷ 8 = 6; 6 × 3 = 18

6 **>, <, >** To find the smaller and larger fraction, make the bottom numbers (the denominators) of each pair of fractions the same. Then compare the top numbers (the numerators), ensuring the small point of the symbol points to the smallest number. For example, $\frac{2}{5} = \frac{8}{20}; \frac{1}{4} = \frac{5}{20}, \frac{8}{20} > \frac{5}{20}$

7–10 To convert a fraction into a percentage, first use an equivalent fraction to make the denominator 100. The numerator is now a percentage.

7 **70%** $\frac{7}{10} = \frac{70}{100} = 70\%$

8 **40%** $\frac{2}{5} = \frac{4}{10} = \frac{40}{100} = 40\%$

9 **75%** $\frac{3}{4} = \frac{15}{20} = \frac{75}{100} = 75\%$

10 **80%, 80%, 32%**
$\frac{8}{10} = \frac{80}{100} = 80\%; \frac{16}{20} = \frac{80}{100} = 80\%; \frac{8}{25} = \frac{32}{100} = 32\%$

11 **5%, $\frac{2}{5}$** To find the numbers that are less than $\frac{1}{2}$ find the decimal and percentage equivalents to $\frac{1}{2}$ and compare whether a card is lower than these equivalents.
For $\frac{5}{7}$, find a fraction equal to $\frac{1}{2}$. This won't work with 7 as a denominator, so use 14: $\frac{7}{14}; \frac{5}{7} = \frac{10}{14}$, which is greater than $\frac{7}{14}$. For $\frac{2}{5}, \frac{5}{10} = \frac{1}{2}$ and $\frac{2}{5} = \frac{4}{10}$, which is less than $\frac{5}{10}$. For the percentages, 50% is equivalent to $\frac{1}{2}$, so 5% is less than $\frac{1}{2}$ but 52% is greater. For the decimals, 0.5 is equivalent to $\frac{1}{2}$, so .52 and 0.7 are both greater than $\frac{1}{2}$.

12 **40%** Count the total number of parts in the circle (10) to find the denominator. The numerator will be the number of parts shaded (4). To convert $\frac{4}{10}$ to a percentage, see Focus test 5, Q7–10.

Focus Test 6: Number sequences
(page 9)

1 **121** First work out the sequence between the given numbers. Then use the same rule to find the missing numbers. In this sequence, the pattern is to subtract 4 each time, so the number after 125 is 121.

2 **c** The numbers in this sequence are decreasing square numbers. 100 is 10 × 10 and 64 is 8 × 8, so the missing number is 81 (9 × 9).

3 **168, 212** The sequence is to add 11 each time: 201 + 11 = 212. To find a missing number before a given number, reverse the operation: 179 − 11 = 168.

4 **8, 9.5** The sequence is to add 1.5 each time. 6.5 + 1.5 = 8 and 8 + 1.5 = 9.5

5 **6360, 6090** The sequence is to subtract 90 each time. 6450 − 90 = 6360 and 6180 − 90 = 6090

6 **704, 352, 22, 11** First follow the rule given, then check the sequence. 44 ÷ 2 = 22 and 22 ÷ 2 = 11. To find previous numbers in the sequence, reverse the operation: 176 × 2 = 352 and 352 × 2 = 704

7 **4.5, 9, 144, 288** 18 ÷ 2 = 9, 9 ÷ 2 = 4.5, 72 × 2 = 144, 144 × 2 = 288

8 **b** Work out the sequence between the numbers to find the rule or pattern: 8279 − 8079 = 200, so the rule is to take away 200.

9 **121** The sequence is increasing squared numbers, so the next number is 121 (11 × 11).

10 **15** The sequence is +2, +3, +4, so 10 + 5 = 15.

11 **+2, +3, +4, +5 or adding consecutive numbers**

12 **636, 648** Add the first and third numbers together and divide by 2 to find the missing number between them: 630 + 642 = 1272 and 1272 ÷ 2 = 636. Then add the third and fifth numbers together and divide by 2 to find the second missing number 642 + 654 = 1296 and 1296 ÷ 2 = 648.

Focus Test 7: Shapes and angles
(pages 10–11)

1 **A, E** A right angle is exactly 90°.

2 **parallelogram** A parallelogram has 2 sets of parallel lines: 2 longer sides of equal length and 2 shorter sides of equal length.

3 **E** A parallelogram has no line of symmetry.

4 **D** A quadrilateral has four sides. D has only 3 sides, making it a triangle.

5 **A = acute, B = obtuse, C = right angle, D = reflex, E = acute, F = acute** A right angle is exactly 90°. An acute angle measures less than 90° and an obtuse angle is more than 90° but less than 180°. A reflex angle is bigger than 180°.

6

Shape	Name	Face	Edges	Vertices
	Square-based pyramid	5	8	5
	Tetrahedron	4	6	4
	Cuboid	6	12	8
	Triangular prism	5	9	6

A face is a flat surface, an edge is a straight line and a vertex is where two edges come together to form a corner.

7 **tetrahedron** A tetrahedron has four triangular faces, six straight edges and four vertices. A tetrahedron may also be referred to as a triangular-based pyramid. The net shows a regular tetrahedron – all 4 faces are equilateral triangles.

8 **triangular prism** A triangular prism has identical triangular faces at each end, three rectangular faces connecting them, and six vertices.

9 **square-based pyramid** A square-based pyramid has a square base, four triangular faces and five vertices.

10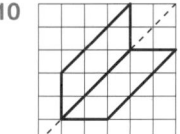

11 **65°**

12 **110°, 90°** To find the missing angle, subtract the given angles from 180°: 180° – 35° – 35° = 110°; 180° – 60° – 30° = 90°.

Focus Test 8: Area and perimeter
(pages 12–13)

1 **27 cm², 21 cm** Multiply the length by the width to find the area: 4.5 cm × 6 cm = 27 cm². The perimeter can be found by adding up the 2 lengths and the 2 widths: 6 cm + 6 cm + 4.5 cm + 4.5 cm = 21 cm.

2 **34 cm², 25 cm** 8.5 cm × 4 cm = 34 cm²; 8.5 cm + 8.5 cm + 4 cm + 4 cm = 25 cm

3 **28 m** The area of the pool is 49 m². Area is length multiplied by width. As the pool is square, each side must be 7 m (7 × 7 = 49). For the perimeter of a square, multiply one side by 4, so 4 × 7 m = 28 m.

4–5 First, count the whole squares and add the half squares, then add the two totals together.

4 **6** There are 4 whole squares and 4 half squares: 4 + (4 ÷ 2) = 6.

5 **10** There are 4 whole squares and 12 half squares: 4 + (12 ÷ 2) = 10.

6 **400 cm²** The area can be found by multiplying the length by the width. In a square, the length and the width are equal: 20 cm × 20 cm = 400 cm².

7 **26 cm** If the width of the rectangle is 4 cm, the length must be 9 cm: 36 ÷ 4 = 9. A rectangle has two pairs of parallel sides of equal length, so add them together to find the perimeter: 4 cm + 4 cm + 9 cm + 9 cm = 26 cm.

8 **32** To find the sides of the rectangle when the length is double the width, add 1 unit (for the width) to 2 units (for the length) to make a group of 3. Divide 24 cm by 3 to find 8. This is the length, so the width is half of this: 8 ÷ 2 = 4. The area is 8 × 4 = 32 cm².

9 **122** To find the area of a compound shape, divide the shape into rectangles, find the area of each rectangle and then add them together: 12 cm × 6 cm = 72 cm²; 10 cm × 5 cm = 50 cm²; 72 cm² + 50 cm² = 122 cm².

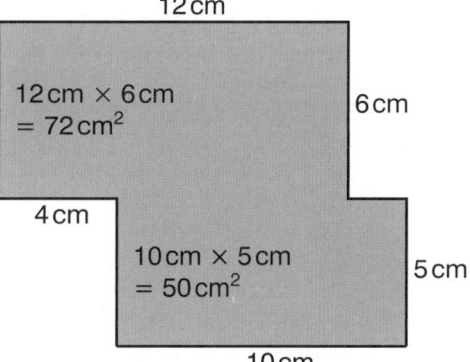

10 **65** To find the area of a shape with a section removed, find the area of the larger shape, then find the area of the smaller shape and subtract the smaller from the larger: 9 cm × 9 cm = 81 cm²; 4 cm × 4 cm = 16 cm²; 81 cm² – 16 cm² = 65 cm².

11 **The areas of A and B are the same** Find the areas by multiplying length by width: 6 m × 6 m = 36 m²; 12 m × 3 m = 36 m².

12 **Shape B** Find the perimeters by adding the lengths of the sides: 6 m + 6 m + 6 m + 6 m = 24 m; 12 m + 12 m + 3 m + 3 m = 30 m.

Focus Test 9: Measures (pages 14–15)

1. **50 ml** To subtract or add measures that have a different scale, first convert between scales so that both scales are the same. 0.75 l = 750 ml; 750 ml – 700 ml = 50 ml
2. **1450 ml** 0.75 l = 750 ml; 750 ml + 700 ml = 1450 ml
3. **70 mm, 7.6 cm, 0.75 m, 78 cm, 7.2 m** To order measurements that have a different scale, first convert between scales so that all are using the same scale. 70 mm = 7 cm; 7.2 m = 720 cm; 0.75 m = 75 cm. Then put them in order.
4. **850 g, 300 g, 1 kg 150 g**
5. **11:07 am** 10:55 am + 12 min = 11:07 am
6.

Arden	09:50	11:28	**13:07**
Blythe	**10:08**	11:46	13:25
Chorton	10:34	**12:12**	13:51
Dunley	10:52	**12:30**	**14:09**

Start with the times given and add or subtract to work out the other times. 11:46 – 11:28 = 18 mins, so 09:50 + 18 mins = 10:08 and 13:25 – 18 mins = 13:07; 13:51 – 13:25 = 26 mins, so 11:46 + 26 mins = 12:12; 10:52 – 10:34 = 18 mins, so 12:12 + 18 mins = 12:30 and 13:51 + 18 mins = 14:09.

7. **8.4 cm** Work out the centimetres first and then the millimetres.
8. **14 cm** If 3 dominoes = 8.4 cm, divide 8.4 by 3 to find the length of 1 domino = 2.8 cm. Now multiply this by 5 to find the length of 5 dominoes: 2.8 × 5 = 14 cm.
9. **23** –9 °C to 0 °C = 9 °C and 0 °C to 14 °C = 14 °C, so 9 °C + 14 °C = 23 °C.
10. **6 kg, 8 kg, 10 kg** First find the weight of box A and box C, which weigh 16 kg together. Box C weighs 4 kg more than Box A, so divide 16 kg in half to make both boxes equal: 16 kg ÷ 2 = 8 kg. Now make Box A 2 kg lighter and Box C 2 kg heavier so that there is a 4 kg difference between them. Box A = 6 kg and Box C = 10 kg. Use this information to find box B: A + B = 14 kg; 6 kg + B = 14 kg; Box B = 8 kg.
11. **260 ml** First turn 1.56 litres into millilitres by multiplying by 1000, then divide by 6: 1.56 × 1000 = 1560 ml; 1560 ÷ 6 = 260.
12. **>, <, <, >** To compare measures that have a different scale, first convert between scales so that both scales are the same. 63 mm = 6.3 cm; 3.06 m = 306 cm; 36 mm = 3.6 cm

Focus Test 10: Transformations and coordinates (pages 16–17)

1. **translation** A translation moves a shape upwards, downwards or side to side, but it does not change its appearance.
2. **reflection** A reflection mirrors a shape's image horizontally, vertically or diagonally.
3. **rotation** A rotation turns a shape in a circle around a fixed point (the centre of rotation). A rotation can rotate clockwise or anticlockwise, often by 90° (a quarter turn), 180° (a half turn) or 270° (a three-quarters turn).

4.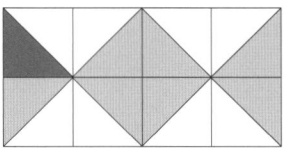

5.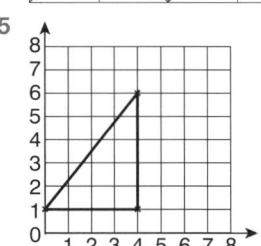

When plotting coordinates on a grid, use the rule "along the corridor and up the stairs" to remember to go horizontal, then vertical.

6. **(2, 2), (2, 3), (3, 3), (3, 4)** Plot the given coordinates and check whether they fit inside the triangle.
7. **(4, 2)** To find the missing coordinate, find the number of squares between B and C and make sure there is the same number of squares between A and D. As B and C are on the same y-axis, then A and D will also be on the same y-axis. B – C = 3 squares to the right; A + 3 squares to the right = 4. A is 2 on the y-axis, so D will also be 2.

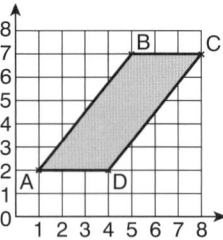

8. **(4, 5), (7, 5), (3, 0)** Vertex A is moved from 1 to 0 on the x-axis, which is –1. Vertex A is moved from 2 to 0 on the y-axis, which is –2. Translate every vertex by (–1, –2) to find their new positions.

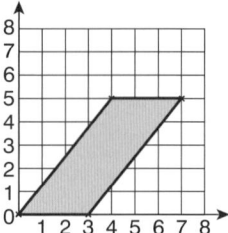

9 **(11, 12)** To find a missing coordinate of a square, match the x-axis of the coordinates above with the y-axis of the coordinate to the side. The x-axis coordinate of the point above the missing one is 11, so the missing x-axis coordinate must also be 11. The y-axis coordinate of the point to the side of the missing one is 12, so the missing y-axis coordinate must also be 12.

10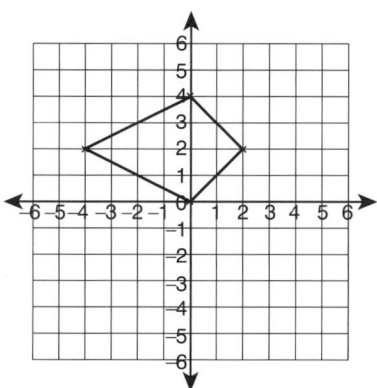

11 **True** Draw the central line of symmetry and check if these coordinates are on that line.

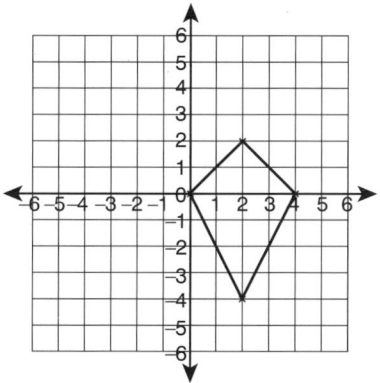

12 **(4, 0)** See Q11 image.

Focus Test 11: Charts, graphs and tables (pages 18–19)

1 **6** Count the number of crosses in the 150–159 row.
2 **14** Count the number of crosses in the shoe size 3 and 4 columns.
3 **6** Count the number of crosses in the shoe size 4 column that are in the 120–129 and 130–139 rows.
4 **12** Count the number of crosses in the shoe sizes 5 and 6 columns that are also in the 130–139, 140–149 and 150–158 rows.
5 **35 minutes** Count the number of 5-minute slots where the bus does not move (shown by a horizontal line).
6 **1 mile** Check that the increments in the distance (miles) is 2 miles for each square. As the bus moves half a square along that axis, the miles completed must be 1.
7 **34 miles** Read off the horizontal line at the bus station.
8 **3:35 pm, 4:55 pm** Compare the timetable to the graph. The bus leaves Bodham at 3:15 and the next stop is Canby. The graph shows that the bus reaches the stop at 3:30 pm and leaves 5 minutes later at 3:35 pm. When the bus leaves Greatley at 4:30 pm, the next stop is Heathend. The bus reaches the stop at 4:50 pm and leaves 5 minutes later at 4:55 pm.
9 **0.5 cm** or $\frac{1}{2}$ **cm** Look at the increments on the y-axis to find that each square represents 2 cm. Between 1:00 and 1:30, the shadow is a quarter of a square, which represents 0.5 cm.
10 **9:15 am** Find 21 cm on the y-axis and follow the horizontal line across to the shadow line. This is halfway between 9:00 am and 9:30 am, which is 9:15 am.
11 **9:00–9:30** Find the length of shadow over the given times. From 9:00–9:30 the shadow length decreased from 24 cm to 18.5 cm, a 5.5 cm decrease. From 9:30–10:00 the shadow length decreased from 18.5 cm to 14.5 cm, a 4 cm decrease. From 10:00–10:30 the shadow length decreased from 14.5 cm to 10.5 cm, a 3 cm decrease. With this type of question, it is not so important to be precise within a centimetre as it is to be comparative.
12 **4 cm** Compare the shadow line at 2:00 (1 cm) to 3:00 (5 cm), which is an increase of 4 cm.

Focus Test 12: Mean, median, mode and probability (pages 20–21)

1 **22** To find the mean, add up the numbers and then divide by the number of numbers: 13 + 39 + 18 + 21 + 29 = 110; 110 ÷ 5 = 22.
2 **21** To find the median, put the numbers in order from smallest to largest and find the middle number: 13, 18, **21**, 29, 29.
3 **29** To find the mode, find the number that is used the most often: 13, **29**, 18, 21, **29**.
4 **2, 2, 3, 3, 4, 7** The number 2 can be put into place, as it is the lowest. The range is the difference between the smallest number and the largest, so if the lowest number is 2 and the range is 5, the highest number must be 7. The modes are 2 and 3, with each appearing twice, so put those in place. Now use the mean to find the missing number. The mean is 3.5 and there are 6 numbers. 3.5 × 6 = 21, so the 6 numbers must add up to 21. Subtract the 5 numbers that you already have from 21 to find the missing number: 21 − 2 − 2 − 3 − 3 − 7 = 4.

5. **2p** There are more 2p coins than any other type.
6. **15p** Add up all the values and then divide by the number of coins: 180p ÷ 12 coins = 15.
7. **10p** Put the values in order from smallest to largest and find the middle number or numbers: 2p, 2p, 2p, 2p, 2p, **10p, 10p**, 10p, 20p, 20p, 50p, 50p (10p + 10p = 20p; 20p ÷ 2 = 10p).
8. **44kg** Add up all the weights and divide by the number of parcels: 47kg + 39kg + 44kg + 53kg + 34kg + 47kg = 264kg; 264kg ÷ 6 = 44kg.
9. **47kg** Find the weight that appears most often: **47kg**, 39kg, 44kg, 53kg, 34kg, **47kg**.
10. **3 blue, 3 green, 2 red or 2 blue, 2 green, 4 red** Make sure there are an equal number of blues and greens.
11. **likely, impossible, even chance, unlikely** Check each statement against the numbers on the spinners using $\frac{3}{6}$ $\left(\frac{1}{2}\right)$ as an even chance. Odd numbers on Spinner A = $\frac{3}{5}$, so this outcome is likely. Spinning a 6 on Spinner A is impossible as there is no 6. Odd number on Spinner B = $\frac{3}{6}$ $\left(\frac{1}{2}\right)$, so that is an even chance. A multiple of 3 on Spinner B = $\frac{2}{6}$, so this outcome is unlikely.
12. **impossible** There are no number 7s on a normal 1–6 dice, so it is impossible.

Mixed Paper 1 (pages 22–25)

1–4 Work to the left from the ones column to the tens, hundreds and thousands column.
 1 22②222
 2 ⑥66 666
 3 111 ①11
 4 4④4 444

5–8

+	0.365	1.74
12.6	**12.965**	**14.34**
4.605	4.97	**6.345**

Subtract 0.365 from 4.97 to find 4.605. Add 4.605 to 1.74 to find 6.345. Add 12.6 to 0.365 to find 12.965. Add 12.6 to 1.74 to find 14.34.

9–12 To solve this type of problem, work out both sides of the equation and then compare them.
 9 **>** 7 × 4 = 28 and 3 × 9 = 27 so 28 > 27
 10 **=** 6 × 6 = 36 and 9 × 4 = 36 so 36 = 36
 11 **<** 49 ÷ 7 = 7 and 48 ÷ 6 = 8 so 7 < 8
 12 **>** 56 ÷ 8 = 7 and 54 ÷ 9 = 6 so 7 > 6
13 **130** Multiply both numbers by 100 to find a whole number as the divider ((45.5 ÷ 0.35) × 100 = 4550 ÷ 35). Then use bus stop division to solve this (see Focus test 3, Q4).
14 **27** Look for a number that appears in the 3 times table.
15 **28** Find a number that appears in both the 7 and 2 times tables.
16 **29** Find a number that can only be divided by 1 and itself.
17 **28** Find a number that fits exactly into 84.
18 $\frac{43}{60}$ Turn the mixed numbers into top-heavy fractions. Next, find a common denominator for both fractions. Finally, subtract the numerators $2\frac{13}{20} = \frac{53}{20} = \frac{159}{60}$; $1\frac{14}{15} = \frac{29}{15} = \frac{116}{60}$; $\frac{159}{60} - \frac{116}{60} = \frac{43}{60}$
19 **286** To find 72% of 300, divide 300 by 100 to find 1%, then multiply by 72 (300 ÷ 100 = 3; 3 × 72 = 216). To find $\frac{5}{6}$ of 84, divide 84 by 6 and then multiply by 5 (84 ÷ 6 = 14; 14 × 5 = 70). Finally, add the two numbers together (216 + 70 = 286).
20–21 See Focus test 5, Q2.
 20 **70%** 0.7 = 0.70 = 70%
 21 **15%** 0.15 = 15%
22–25 See Focus test 6, Q1.
 22 **6.2** The sequence is to add 1.5 each time, so 4.7 + 1.5 = 6.2.
 23 **25** This sequence is descending square numbers. 36 = 6^2, so the next number must be 5^2 = 25.
 24 **1.5** The sequence is to add 3.6 each time, so −2.1 + 3.6 = 1.5.
 25 **120** This sequence is to multiply by 2 each time, so 60 × 2 = 120.

26–29

Shape name	Number of vertices	Number of edges
Pentagonal-based pyramid	6	10
Hexagonal prism	12	18

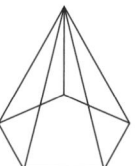

30 **9** There is a difference between the length and width of the grey shaded sections of 3cm (8cm − 5cm = 3cm), so the central square is 3cm × 3cm = 9cm².
31 **160** The large square is 13cm × 13cm = 169cm² (5cm + 8cm for each side). The central square is 9cm², so the shaded area is 169cm² − 9cm² = 160cm².
32 **2** The two sides of the square must be the same and multiplied together make 4, so the sides must be 2m (2m × 2m = 4m).

33 **a** The perimeter of the window is 120 cm + 325 cm + 120 cm + 325 cm = 890 cm.
34 **2:18** The present time is 2:03, so adding 15 minutes = 2:18.
35 **15** The top temperature is −6 °C so adding 6 °C takes the temperature to 0 °C. The bottom temperature is 9 °C, so 9 °C + 6 °C = 15 °C.
36–37 See Focus test 9, Q12.
36 **>** 33.3 km = 33 300 m, which is larger than 3300 m.
37 **=** 0.06 l = 60 ml, which is the same.
38 **reflection** See Focus test 10, Q2. This is a reflection with a vertical mirror line.
39 **rotation** See Focus test 10, Q3. This triangle has been rotated clockwise by 90° (a quarter turn).
40 **translation** See Focus test 10, Q1. This triangle has moved upwards and to the right.
41 **False** The coordinates (1,0) and (2,3) are on the line but not (6,3).
42 **30 km** Find 10:30 from the *x*-axis and imagine a line travelling upwards until it meets the graph. Reading the distance from the *y*-axis, the distance covered is 30 km.
43 **2:30** Find 55 km from the *y*-axis and travel to the right until it meets the graph. Reading the time from the *x*-axis, the time is 2:30.
44 **2 hours** Look for the sections of the journey where the line is horizontal, which shows the distance not changing. These are the periods of rest. The cyclist remains at rest between 10:30 and 11:00 (30 mins), 12:30 and 1:30 (1 hour) and 3:30 and 4:00 (30 mins) which is a total of 2 hours.
45 **90 km** Read off the total journey at the end to find 90 km.
46 **150 cm** See Focus test 12, Q2. The heights in order are 145, 148, 149, **150**, 152, 152, 157.
47 **152 cm** See Focus test 12, Q3. In this list, 152 appears twice and the other numbers appear only once.
48 **150 cm** See Focus test 12, Q1. 157 + 152 + 148 + 145 + 152 + 150 + 149 = 1053 and 1053 ÷ 7 = 150.42. This is 150 cm to the nearest cm.
49 **poor chance** Impossible is throwing a zero or over 6. Certain is to throw any number between 1 and 6. Even chance is to throw an odd or an even number. A 6 is not impossible, but not as good as an even chance, so there is a poor chance of throwing a 6.
50 **certain** A dice will show a number between 1 and 6 so it is certain that you will throw a number less than 7.

Mixed Paper 2 (pages 25–29)

1–4 Place the numbers on a decimal grid. To make a number larger by 100, find the hundreds column and make the number 1 larger. When the number in the hundreds column is already 9, adding 1 makes the number 10, so put 0 in the hundreds column and add 1 in the thousands column.
1 **78 045**
2 **51 082**
3 **17 000**
4 **38 299**
5 **106 175** Write each number out in figures and then add them together.

	HTh	TTh	Th	H	T	U
		5	7	2	6	9
+		4	8	9	0	6
	1	0	6	1	7	5
			1	1		1

6 **4435** Write each number out in figures and then subtract.

	TTh	Th	H	T	U
	1	12	12	11	1
−	2	3	3	2	3
	1	8	8	8	8
	0	4	4	3	5

7 **1.001, 1.011, 1.101, 1.2, 10.01** See Focus test 1, Q11.
8 **£2.45** First find the price of three of each of the items using a suitable multiplication method. Then find the total cost by adding these three subtotals together.
Alternatively, add together one of each item and multiply by 3.
Finally subtract this total cost from £20.
9 **1 236 895** As the number must be divisible by 5, take the 5 out of order and put it at the end. Then fill in the rest of the digits, starting with the smallest digit on the far left and working towards the right.
10 **53** Multiply the numbers, then add on the remainder (12 × 4 = 48; 48 + 5 = 53). Then work through the equation to check that it is correct.
11 **6** Solve the 8 × 30 first (8 × 30 = 240), then divide this by 40 (240 ÷ 40 = 6). Work through the equation to check that it is correct.
12–13 To multiply decimal numbers, solve the multiplication while ignoring the decimal point. Then count the number of digits after the decimal point in the question, and make sure the answer has the same number of digits after the decimal point.
12 **2.7** 0.3 × 9 = 3 × 9 = 27. There is one digit after the decimal point (the 3), so 2.7 must be the answer.

13 **0.252** 0.84 × 0.3 Make each number a whole number to carry out the multiplication. Then count how many spaces you moved the decimal digits. 84 × 3 = 252. There are three digits after the decimal point (the 8, 4 and 3) so 0.252 must be the answer.

14–19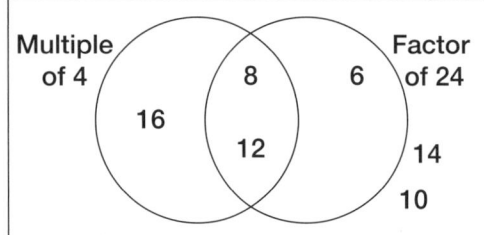

First find the multiples of 4 and then the factors of 24. Find the common numbers and place them into the middle space shared by both circles. The space on the left has all of the multiples of 4 that are not shared and the space on the right circle has all of the factors of 24 that are not shared. The numbers 10 and 14 are neither multiples of 4 nor factors of 24, so they must go outside of the circles.

20–21 See Focus test 5, Q3.
20 $\frac{4}{5}$ 0.8 = $\frac{8}{10}$ = $\frac{4}{5}$
21 $6\frac{3}{4}$ 6.75 = $6\frac{75}{100}$ = $6\frac{3}{4}$

22–23 See Focus test 5, Q6.
22 > $\frac{2}{5}$ = $\frac{6}{15}$; $\frac{6}{15}$ > $\frac{5}{15}$
23 = $\frac{3}{4}$ = $\frac{9}{12}$; $\frac{9}{12}$ = $\frac{9}{12}$

24 **392** Follow the rule of the sequence: (52 + 144) × 2 = 392.
25 **64** Follow the rule of the sequence: (8 × 16) ÷ 2 = 64.

26–27 See Focus test 6, Q1.
26 **–5.5** The rule of the sequence is to add 4.7 each time.
27 **–1.95** The rule of the sequence is to subtract 3.54 each time.
28 **Regular hexagon** A regular hexagon has 6 sides of equal length and 6 lines of symmetry, running between each pair of vertices and between the halfway points between vertices.
29 **Rectangle** A rectangle has 4 right angles, 2 pairs of different length sides and 2 lines of symmetry, vertical and horizontal.
30 **Tetrahedron** A tetrahedron is a solid, 3-D shape with 4 triangular faces, 6 edges and 4 vertices.
31 **Cylinder** A cylinder has no vertices, 2 edges and 2 circular faces.
32 **75** See Focus test 8, Q1. 7.5m × 10m = 75m².

33 **35** See Focus test 8, Q1. 7.5m + 10m + 7.5m + 10m = 35m.
34–35 **8, 4** Look for pairs of numbers that can be multiplied together to make 32, then choose the pair in which one number is half the size of the other (1 × 32, 2 × 16, **4 × 8**).
36 **A** In scale A, the arrow is between 40 and 41 kg. In scale B, the arrow is between 39 and 40 kg, so scale A shows the heavier weight.
37 **80.25** Scale A is 40.5 kg and scale B is 39.75 kg, so add them together (40.5 kg + 39.75 kg = 80.25 kg).
38 **17.89kg** See Focus test 9, Q1. (0.75 kg = 750 g; 3.2 kg = 3200 g; 12.5 kg = 12 570 g).

				1	2	0
			1	2	5	0
				7	5	0
+			3	2	0	0
		1	2	5	7	0
		1	7	8	9	0
			1	1		

39 **C** See Focus test 10, Q3. The first flag has been rotated clockwise by 90°.
40 **C** See Focus test 10, Q2. The first triangle has been reflected along a vertical mirror line to make triangle C.
41 **(–2, 5)** When finding coordinates on a grid, use the rule "along the corridor and up the stairs" to remember to go horizontal, then vertical.
42

Another good way of remembering the order for coordinates is that x comes before y in the alphabet.
43 **130** Find the coats line in the y-axis. Follow the chequered men's line and read the numbers above to find 130.
44 **40** Find the shoes line in the y-axis. Follow the chequered men's line and read the numbers above to find 250. Do the same with the women's line to find 290, then subtract (290 – 250 = 40).
45 **350** Find the jumpers line in the y-axis. Follow the chequered men's line and read the numbers above to find 150. Do the same with the women's line to find 200, then add them together (150 + 200 = 350).

46 **true** Find the hats line in the *y*-axis. Follow the dark grey men's line to see that it is longer than the women's line. Now look at the other pairs of lines to see if there are any other pairs where the dark grey men's line is longer than the solid women's line. There are none, so the statement is true.

47 **16** See Focus test 12, Q1. 14 + 15 + 18 + 14 + 19 = 80; 80 ÷ 5 = 16

48 **15** See Focus test 12, Q2. The scores in order are 14, 14, **15**, 18, 19.

49 **14** See Focus test 12, Q3. 14 appears twice on the list but the other numbers appear only once.

50 **5** To find the range, subtract the smallest number from the largest number (19 – 14 = 5).

Mixed Paper 3 (pages 29–34)

1–5 **4000, 3000, 4000, 4000, 2000** See Focus test 1, Q12.

6 **28.042** See Focus test 2, Q4–5.

	1	6	•	7	9	2
		4	•	3	0	0
+		6	•	0	0	0
		0	•	9	5	0
	2	8	•	0	4	2
	1	2		1		

7 **8.01, 4.41** First divide 12.42 by 2 to make both A and B equal (12.42 ÷ 2 = 6.21). To make a difference of 3.6, find half of that amount (3.6 ÷ 2 = 1.8), then add 1.8 to one number to find A and subtract 1.8 from the other to find B (6.21 + 1.8 = 8.01; 6.21 – 1.8 = 4.41).

8 **A = 5, B = 6, C = 7** The possible combinations are 123, 234, 345, 456, 567, 678 and 789. Start by looking at the ones column. C and A must add together to make either 2 or 12. They can't make 2, because the only possible combination is 1 + 1, and C and A cannot be the same number. The possible pairs that would add up to 12 are 3 + 9, 4 + 8 and 5 + 7. Because A, B and C are three consecutive numbers, 5 + 7 is the only pair that works (A = 5 and C = 7). Now look at the tens column, where B and A add up to 11 (remember that the 1 has been carried over from the units column). If A = 5, B must be 6. Fill in all the digits to check that the sum works (567 + 655 = 1222).

9 **1 drink = £1.80, 1 sandwich = £3.75, 1 cake = £1.20** The bills for Table 1 and Table 2 are the same except for 1 cake. Find the cost of 1 cake by subtracting (£13.50 – £12.30 = £1.20). Next take away the 4 cakes from Table 3 (£19.50 – £4.80 = £14.70). The remaining £14.70 is the same as Tables 1 and 2 except there are 2 more drinks. Find the cost of 2 drinks by subtracting the cake from Table 1 (£12.30 – £1.20 = £11.10) and then subtracting this from Table 3's food and drink (£14.70 – £11.10 = £3.60). Divide this answer by 2 to find the cost of 1 drink (£3.60 ÷ 2 = £1.80). Finally, take Table 1 and remove the cake and 2 drinks to find the cost of 2 sandwiches (£12.30 – £1.20 – £1.80 – £1.80 = £7.50). Divide the answer by 2 to find the cost of 1 sandwich (£7.50 ÷ 2 = £3.75).

10–13

IN	150	**240**	360	450	**600**
OUT	**5**	8	**12**	15	20

To find the OUT numbers, take the IN number and divide by 30 (150 ÷ 30 = 5). To solve the IN numbers, take the OUT number and multiply by 30 (8 × 30 = 240).

14–15 **29, 59** A prime number is any number that can only be divided by itself or 1.

16 **112** Think about the 8 times table and start with 96 (8 × 12), then add 8 until the answer is between 110 and 120 (96 + 8 = 104; 104 + 8 = 112).

17 **12** Find the factors of 60, then select one that is smaller than 15, but larger than 10 (1 × 60, 2 × 30, 3 × 20, 4 × 15, 5 × **12**, 6 × 10).

18 $\frac{12}{40}$ **38% 0.49 72% 0.76** $\frac{16}{20}$ To compare numbers, they must all be in the same format. To convert a fraction into a percentage, first use an equivalent fraction to make the denominator 100. The numerator is now a percentage ($\frac{16}{20} = \frac{80}{100} = 80\%$; $\frac{12}{40} = \frac{6}{20} = \frac{30}{100} = 30\%$). To find a percentage from a decimal, place the decimal numbers into hundredths, then take the tenths and hundredths to form the percentage (0.76 = 76%; 0.49 = 49%). The numbers can now be placed in order.

19 **£16.40, £19.68, £13.12** Calculate 1% of the original sale price and multiply it by 18. Then, subtract this discount from the original price to find the sale price.
Book 1: £20.00 ÷ 100 = 0.20; 0.20 × 18 = £3.60; £20.00 – £3.60 = **£16.40**
Book 2: £24.00 ÷ 100 = 0.24; 0.24 × 18 = £4.32; £24.00 – £4.32 = **£19.68**
Book 3: £16.00 ÷ 100 = 0.16; 0.16 × 18 = £2.88; £16.00 – £2.88 = **£13.12**

20 **9** To find a fraction of a number, divide the number by the denominator and then multiply the answer by the numerator ($\frac{3}{16}$ of 32 = 32 ÷ 16 = 2 and 2 × 3 = 6). There were 6 children absent from Class 1 on Monday and half as

many on Tuesday (6 ÷ 2 = 3). Working out the number of children absent from Class 2 requires finding a percentage of a number. To find 10% of 30, divide 30 by 10 (30 ÷ 10 = 3). There were 3 children absent on Monday and double that number on Tuesday (3 × 2 = 6). Add the Tuesday totals for Class 1 and Class 2 (6 + 3 = 9).

21 **292** Subtract these numbers from the total number of students in the class to find the total number of children in class on Monday and Tuesday. It may be helpful to put the numbers in a table before adding them all together to find the total number of children in school for the week:

	Mon	Tue	Wed	Thu	Fri	TOTAL
Class 1	26	29	32	32	32	151
Class 2	27	24	30	30	30	141
						292

22 **b** See Focus test 6, Q1. In this sequence, the number added increases by 1 each time (41 + 9 = 50; 50 + 10 = 60; 60 + 11 = 71; 71 + 12 = 83).

23 **d** Work out the sequence between the numbers to find the rule. From 0 to 2.5 is +2.5; from 2.5 to 5 is +2.5, from 5 to 7.5 is +2.5 and from 7.5 to 10 is +2.5.

24 **28.1, −3.4** See Focus test 6, Q1. From 59.6 to 49.1 is −10.5 and from 49.1 to 38.6 is also −10.5, so the rule is subtract 10.5. Now it is possible to find the missing numbers (38.6 − 10.5 = 28.1; 7.1 − 10.5 = −3.4).

25 $6\frac{9}{10}$ To find the pattern of fractions, make each fraction equivalent so that the bottom numbers (the denominators) are the same. Then compare the top numbers (the numerators). This shows that the sequence is that each fraction subtracts 1 whole number and $\frac{1}{10}$ each time ($6\frac{9}{10}$, $5\frac{8}{10}$ ($5\frac{4}{5}$), $4\frac{7}{10}$, $3\frac{6}{10}$ ($3\frac{3}{5}$), $2\frac{5}{10}$ ($2\frac{1}{2}$), $1\frac{4}{10}$ ($1\frac{2}{5}$))

26 **Cuboid** A cuboid is a solid shape with six rectangular faces.

27 **55**

28 **D** A regular polygon has equal length sides and equal sized angles. Shape D is a regular pentagon.

29–30

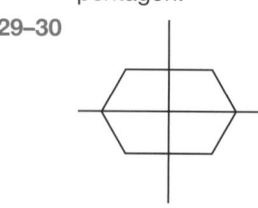

31–32 The area of a square is the length of a side multiplied by itself.

31 **28** 7 × 7 = 49 so each side must be 7 cm and the perimeter is 4 × 7 cm = 28 cm.

32 **12** 3 × 3 = 9 so each side must be 3 cm and the perimeter = 4 × 3 cm = 12 cm.

33 **38** See Focus test 8, Q1. 7 m + 12 m + 7 m + 12 m = 38 m

34 **84** See Focus test 8, Q1. 7 m × 12 m = 84 m²

35–36 Read off the measurement scale, looking first between the litres and then at the increments of millilitres.

35 **2600**

36 **1750**

37 **850 ml** 2600 ml − 1750 ml = 850 ml

38 **4.35** 1750 ml + 2600 ml = 4350 ml, but the answer must be given in litres, so divide by 1000 (4250 ÷ 1000 = 4.35).

39–40

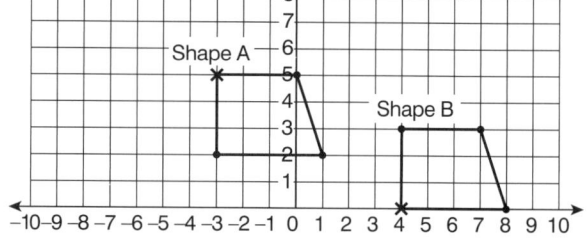

41 **Translation** See Focus test 10, Q1. Shape A has moved down and to the right to form shape B.

42 **(0, 5)** Try each coordinate until there is a match.

43 **2** 1.6 m = 160 cm, so locate the height measurement of 161 cm or over to find 2 squares.

44 **141 cm–150 cm** See Focus test 12, Q3. Find the mode by looking at which height range has the tallest bar.

45 **8** Add together the squares for 130 cm or under and 131–140 cm.

46 **25** Add together the number of squares.

47 **even chance** Half of the balloons are yellow, so there is an even chance of bursting a yellow balloon.

48 **unlikely** As 4 of the balloons are red, there is more chance for another coloured balloon to be burst, so it is less than even chance, but it is not impossible. It is therefore unlikely.

49 **likely** As there are 2 green balloons, there is more than an even chance that a burst balloon is another colour but it is not certain, so there is a likely chance.

50 **impossible** As there are no blue balloons, it is impossible for a blue balloon to burst.

Mixed Paper 4 (pages 34–38)

1–4 **4.06, 4.55, 5.4, 5.82** There are 20 increments between 4 and 6 and each increment has been divided into 10. Put the number 5 at the halfway mark, then work out the whole numbers. Then count the larger increments to provide the number in the tenths column. Finally, count the smallest increments to find the number in the hundredths column.

5–6 See Focus test 2, Q4–5.

Shopping receipt A

	0	0	•	7	6
	0	1	•	3	8
	0	0	•	2	3
	0	4	•	9	9
	1	0	•	1	2
+	0	0	•	1	4
	1	7	•	6	2
		2		3	

Shopping receipt B

		2	•	9	9
	1	3	•	9	4
		3	•	5	0
		1	•	9	5
		0	•	5	6
+		0	•	8	2
		2	3	•	7	6
		1	4		2	

5 **£6.14** £23.76 − £17.62 = £6.14

6 **£8.62** £23.76 + £17.62 = £41.38; £50.00 − £41.38 = £8.62

7 **2918** Find the distance on the chart and double it to find the length of the return journey (1459 × 2 = 2918).

8 **4098** 5557 km − 1459 km = 4098 km

9–10 See Mixed paper 2, Q12–13.

9 **0.456** First solve the multiplication (38 × 12 = 456). There are 3 digits after the decimal point so the answer must move 3 places to the right.

10 **34.568** First solve the multiplication (4321 × 8 = 34 568). There are 3 digits after the decimal point (2, 1, 8), so the answer must also move 3 places to the right.

11 **6** Divide 450 by 8 (450 ÷ 8 = 56.25) and then round it up to the nearest whole number, which is 57. Finally, multiply 8 by 57 and subtract 450 from this to find the smallest number that we can add to 450 to make it exactly divisible by 8 (57 × 8 = 456; 456 − 450 = 6).

12 **119** To find one third of a number, divide by the denominator and multiply by the numerator (357 ÷ 3 = 119; 119 × 1 = 119).

13–14 **56, 91** A multiple of 7 can be divided by 7, leaving no remainder.

15–16 **(3, 18)** A pair of factors are numbers that multiply to fit exactly into another number (3 × 18 = 54).

17–18 To turn an improper fraction to a mixed number, divide the denominator into the numerator and leave the remaining number as a fraction.

17 $3\frac{1}{2}$ 7 ÷ 2 = 3 + $\frac{1}{2}$

18 $2\frac{2}{5}$ 12 ÷ 5 = 2 + $\frac{2}{5}$

19 **15** See Mixed paper 3, Q14–15. 15 can be divided by 1, 15, 3 and 5, so it is not a prime number.

20 **47** The sequence is to add 4 each time, so adding on multiples of 4 from the starting number of 23, up to the number 50 means that 47 is the highest number that does not go over 50.

21 **0.10101** The numbers are multiplying by 10 each time, so working backwards from 1.0101, divide by 10.

22 **+2, +3, +4, etc. each time** The sequence rule is +2, +3, +4, +5, etc. (from 1 to 3 = +2; from 3 to 6 = +3; from 6 to 10 = +4, and so on).

23 **36 dots** The pattern of dots to row numbers are:

Row	1	2	3	4	5	6	7	8	9	10	11	12
Dots	1	3	6	10	15	21	28	36	45	55	66	78

24 **12 rows**

25 **66** There are 180° in a triangle and, in an isosceles triangle, two angles are the same. Subtract the known angle from 180° (180° − 48° = 132°), then divide by 2 to find x (132 ÷ 2 = 66).

26 **sometimes** Triangles such as equilateral and isosceles triangles are symmetrical but right angled and scalene triangles are not.

27 **120**

28–29 **109 m²** See Focus test 8, Q9. The shape on the left is 12 m × 7 m = 84 m² and the shape on the right is 5 m × 5 m = 25 m². Add the two areas together (84 m² + 25 m² = 109 m²).

29 **436** To find the number of tiles needed, first work out that each tile is half a metre by half a metre. So for the 12 m length, you can fit 24 tiles across. For the 7 m length you can fit 14 tiles up. Do the same for the 5 m by 5 m square. You can fit 10 tiles across by 10 tiles up. Marking in how many tiles fit across and up can be helpful for these kinds of question. Multiply to find the area in tiles for each section (24 × 14 = 336 tiles; 10 × 10 = 100 tiles) and add together the rectangle and square (336 + 100 = 436).

30 **Room A** Room A is 7 m × 8 m = 56 m² and Room B is 9 m × 6 m = 54 m².

31 **The perimeters of room A and B are the same length.** Room A has the perimeter 7 m + 8 m + 7 m + 8 m = 30 m and Room B has the perimeter 6 m + 9 m + 6 m + 9 m = 30 m.

32–34 **146 cm, 3000 mm, 14.5 m, 0.32 km, 450 000 mm, 1.6 km** See Focus test 9, Q1. In this list, 1.6 km = 1600 m; 3000 mm = 3 m; 146 cm = 1.46 m; 0.32 km = 320 m; 450 000 mm = 450 m.

35 **2 litres** First multiply the 12 litres by 1000 to find 12 000 ml. Then multiply the 20 cups by

300 ml to find 6000 ml. Next, multiply the 40 ladles by 100 ml to find 4000 ml. Then, subtract the cups and ladles from the full bucket (12 000 ml – 6000 ml – 4000 ml = 2000 ml). Finally, divide by 1000 to find the answer in litres (2000 ÷ 1000 = 2).

36–39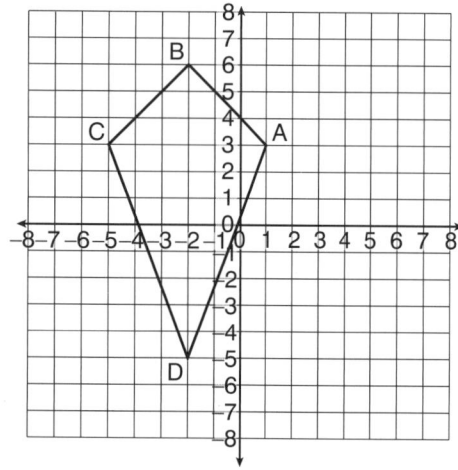

40 **Kite** A kite has vertical symmetry, one pair of matching angles, and adjacent pairs of sides are equal in length.
41 **1** A kite has 1 line of vertical symmetry.
42 **acute** An acute angle is any angle less than 90°.
43 **600 grams** Follow the bottom scale to the far right to find 20 ounces, then read the conversion above to find 600 grams.
44 **15 ounces** Follow the top scale to the middle of 400 and 500 grams, then read the conversion below to find 15 ounces.
45–46 **150, 300** Follow the bottom scale to find 5 ounces and then read the conversion above to find 150 grams of butter. Follow the bottom scale to find 10 ounces and then read the conversion above to find 300 grams of flour.
47 **44 kg** See Focus test 12, Q1. 57 kg + 39 kg + 28 kg + 84 kg + 15 kg + 41 kg = 264 kg; 264 kg ÷ 6 = 44 kg
48 **40 kg** See Focus test 12, Q2. The weights in order are 15 kg, 28 kg, **39 kg, 41 kg**, 57 kg, 84 kg. If the number of numbers is even, there will be two numbers sharing the middle. Add them together and then divide by 2 to find the median (39 kg + 41 kg = 80 kg; 80 kg ÷ 2 = 40 kg).
49–50 **42 kg, 39 kg** To find the new mean, add another 30 kg to the total and divide by 7 (264 kg + 30 kg = 294 kg; 294 kg ÷ 7 = 42 kg). To find the new median, add 30 kg to the list of ordered weights and find the new middle number (15 kg, 28 kg, 30 kg, **39 kg**, 41 kg, 57 kg, 84 kg).

Mixed Paper 5 (pages 38–41)

1–4 To multiply or divide by 100, place the numbers on a decimal grid. To make a number larger by 100, move the numbers to the left twice. If there is nothing in the ones column, place a zero in it. To make a number smaller by 100, move the numbers to the right twice. If there is nothing in the ones column, place a zero in it.
1 **6** 0.06 × 100 = 6
2 **2310** 23.1 × 100 = 2310
3 **18.06** 1806 ÷ 100 = 18.06
4 **0.72** 72 ÷ 100 = 0.72
5 **8500 m, 9499 m** If the height is rounded to the nearest 1000 m, the smallest number that can be rounded up is 8500 m, as anything less will round down. The largest number that can be rounded down to 9000 m is 9499, as anything greater will round up.
6 **8450 m, 8549 m** If the height is rounded to the nearest 100 m, the smallest number that can be rounded up is 8450 m, as anything less will round down. The largest number that can be rounded down to 8500 m is 8549, as anything greater will round up.
7 **7150, 7249** If the height is rounded to the nearest 1000 m, Mount Khartaphu must be 6500 m–7499 m, but rounded to the nearest 100 m it is 7150 m–7249 m and this is more accurate, as rounding to the nearest 100 m is more precise than to the nearest 1000 m.
8–9 **87.6, 7.3** To find 87.6, multiply the two numbers below (14.6 × 6 = 87.6). To find 7.3, divide the number above by the number to the right (14.6 ÷ 2 = 7.3).
10 **8** Divide £12 by £1.50 to find the kilograms of apples that can be bought.
11–12 **3, 23** Take each of the two large numbers and divide them into 70 to find the closest pair (70 ÷ 17 = 4.12; 70 ÷ 23 = 3.04). This shows that 23 and 3 are the pair that give the number closest to 70.
13 **126** Work backwards and reverse the order of operations to solve this (18 × 42 = 756; 756 ÷ 6 = 126).
14 **4** To find a cubed number, multiply a number by itself and by itself again. $2^3 = 2 \times 2 \times 2 = 8$, $3^3 = 3 \times 3 \times 3 = 27$, $4^3 = 4 \times 4 \times 4 = 64$
15 **17** See Mixed paper 3, Q14–15. 14 can be divided by 2 and 7, 15 can be divided by 3 and 5, and 16 can be divided by 2, 4 and 8. 17 can only be divided by itself and 1.
16–17 **3, 19** The factors of 57 are the pairs of numbers that fit exactly into it (1 × 57, 3 × 19). Written in order they are 1, 3, 19, 57.

18 **450** Start by turning the two fractions into percentages to find that 20% of the passengers are women ($\frac{1}{5} = \frac{2}{10} = \frac{20}{100} = 20\%$) and 30% are men ($\frac{3}{10} = \frac{30}{100} = 30\%$). Next, add up the three percentages to find the total number of men, women and girls (20% + 30% + 40% = 90%). The remaining percentage is 10%, which will be the boys. There are 45 boys, so this can be used to find the total numbers of passengers. If 45 boys = 10% then 450 passengers = 100%.

19 **180** Girls make up 40% of the passengers. 45 = 10% so 45 × 4 = 40% = 180 girls.

20 **90** Women make up 20% of the passengers. 45 = 10% so 45 × 2 = 90 women.

21 **135** Men make up 30% of the passengers. 45 = 10% so 45 × 3 = 30% = 135 men.

22–25 See Focus test 6, Q1.

22–23 **92, 101** The sequence is to add 9 each time (83 +9 = 92; 92 +9 = 101).

24–25 **379, 376** The sequence is to subtract 3 each time (382 − 3 = 379; 379 − 3 = 376).

26 **3** A quadrilateral is a 4-sided shape, so A, C and E are quadrilaterals.

27 **2** D and E have no lines of symmetry.

28 **1** A reflex angle is more than 180°, so shape A has a reflex angle inside.

29 **3** An obtuse angle is more than 90° but less than 180°. Shapes B, C and E have obtuse angles.

30 **10** A square has 4 sides of the same length and to find the area, multiply length by width. 10 × 10 = 100, so each side length is 10 cm.

31 **57 m²** See Focus test 8, Q1. 9.5 m × 6 m = 57 m²

32 **31 m** See Focus test 8, Q1. 9.5 m + 6 m + 9.5 m + 6 m = 31 m

33 **320 m** See Focus test 8, Q1. 95 m + 65 m + 95 m + 65 m = 320 m

34–35 **12:07, 13:03** or **1:03 pm** There are 17 minutes between Vale Bus Station and Welbourn Church. 11:50 + 17 mins = 12:07. There are 24 minutes between Yarley School and Zennor Bridge. 12:39 + 24 = 13:03, which can also be written as 1:03 pm.

36 **1 hour 13 minutes** From 11:50 to 13:03 it is 1 hour and 13 minutes.

37 **12:35** 12:39 − 4 mins = 12:35

38–39 **A (−6, 1), B (−6, 4)** Remember that the x-axis is the first coordinate, followed by the y-axis. It may be helpful to remember that x comes before y in the alphabet.

40 **(−5, 3)** Check each coordinate to find that the only one inside the triangle is (−5, 3).

41 **(−2, 8)**

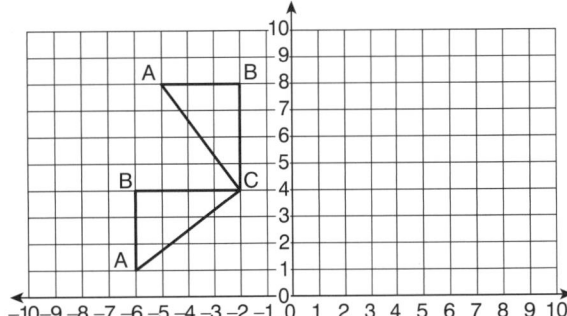

42–45 To solve a Venn diagram, look at the three individual circles and what each one shows. Where the circles overlap, it shows that the children have more than one item of food.

42 **4** Two numbers appear in the section where the Cake and Fruit circles overlap. One of these numbers is also in the Yoghurt circle, so it can't be correct. The remaining number (4) is the answer.

43 **7** The only number in the Fruit circle that doesn't overlap with either of the other circles is 7.

44 **4** There is a place in the centre of the diagram where all three circles overlap, and it shows 4.

45 **18** Add up all the numbers in the Yoghurt circle (3 + 4 + 5 + 6 = 18).

46 **even chance** There are an equal number of odd and even numbers, so there is an even chance of rolling an even number with the dice.

47 **35 cm** See Focus test 12, Q3. **35 cm,** 25 cm, 15 cm, 25 cm, **35 cm, 35 cm,** 15 cm, 25 cm, **35 cm**

48 **25 cm** See Focus test 12, Q2. These measurements in order are: 15 cm, 15 cm, 25 cm, 25 cm, **25 cm,** 35 cm, 35 cm, 35 cm, 35 cm.

49 **20 cm** See Mixed paper 2, Q50. 35 cm − 15 cm = 20 cm

50 **20.5** See Focus test 12, Q1. 19 + 24 + 27 + 12 = 82; 82 ÷ 4 = 20.5

Mixed Paper 6 (pages 42–46)

1–2 (**34.064**), **36.604** See Focus test 1, Q11.

3–4 **1236** First list all of the double-digit numbers between 10 and 15, then multiply each of these by 3. Finally, cross out the numbers with repeated digits.
10 × 3 = 30; ~~10 30~~ (double 0)
11 × 3 = 33; ~~11 33~~ (double 1)
12 × 3 = 36; **12 36**
13 × 3 = 39; ~~13 39~~ (double 3)
14 × 3 = 42; ~~14 42~~ (double 4)
15 × 3 = 45; ~~15 45~~ (double 5)

5 **47.54** Subtract the cost of the chair from the cost of the table (£137.49 − £89.95 = £47.54).
6 **317.39** Add the cost of 1 table to the cost of 2 chairs (£137.49 + £89.95 + £89.95 = £317.39).
7 **42.49** Subtract £95 from the cost of the table (£137.49 − £95.00 = £42.49).
8 **5.05** Subtract the cost of the chair from £95 (£95.00 − £89.95 = £5.05).
9 **26** The area can be found by multiplying the length by the width, so dividing the area by one side will give the other length (234 cm² ÷ 9 cm = 26 cm).
10 **84** Multiply Ryan's age by 6 to find his mother's age (7 × 6 = 42) and then multiply the answer by 2 to find his grandfather's age (42 × 2 = 84).
11 **7200 km** Multiply the bus's daily distance by 5 to find the weekly distance (40 km × 5 = 200 km a week). Then multiply the answer by 12 to find the distance in 1 term (200 km × 12 = 2400 km a term) and multiply this answer by 3 to find the yearly distance (2400 × 3 = 7200 km per year).
12 **255** First divide the total number of sandwiches by 4 to find out how many people are at the wedding party (340 ÷ 4 = 85 people). Then multiply the total number of people by 3 to find out how many tomatoes will be needed (85 × 3 = 255 tomatoes).

13–16

	A factor of 72	Not a factor of 72
A multiple of 8	24	48
Not a multiple of 8	36	60

24 is a multiple of 8 AND a factor of 72. 48 is a multiple of 8 but is NOT a factor of 72. 36 is NOT a multiple of 8 but it IS a factor of 72. 60 is NOT a multiple of 8 and is NOT a factor of 72.

17–18 **0.2, $\frac{1}{5}$** To convert a decimal into a percentage, see Focus test 5, Q2 (0.2 = 0.20 = 20%; 0.5 = 0.50 = 50%; 0.02 = 2%). To convert a fraction into a percentage, see Focus test 5, Q7 ($\frac{2}{5} = \frac{40}{100} = 40\%$; $\frac{1}{5} = \frac{20}{100} = 20\%$).

19–20 **$\frac{7}{8}, \frac{1}{2}$** See Focus test 5, Q1. $\frac{1}{2} = \frac{4}{8}$; $\frac{4}{8} + \frac{3}{8} = \frac{7}{8}$; $\frac{1}{5} = \frac{2}{10}$; $\frac{7}{10} - \frac{2}{10} = \frac{5}{10}$ or $\frac{1}{2}$.

21 **46** The first square uses 4 sticks, and each additional square is adding on 3 sticks, so for 15 squares there are 46 sticks.

Squares:	1	2	3	4	5	6	7	8	9	10	11	12	13	14	15
Sticks:	4	7	10	13	16	19	22	25	28	31	34	37	40	43	46

22–23 See Focus test 6, Q1.
22 **7.6** In this sequence, the pattern is to subtract 1.2 each time, so the number after 8.8 is 7.6 (8.8 − 1.2 = 7.6).
23 **510** In this sequence, the pattern is to add 150 each time, so the number after 360 is 510 (360 +150 = 510).
24 **41** Write out the sequence for each instrument until there is a common number between them all.
Drum: 1, 5, 9, 13, 17, 21, 25, 29, 33, 37, **41**
Cymbal: 1, 6, 11, 16, 21, 26, 31, 36, **41**
Bell: 1, 3, 5 ... The bell plays on all the odd numbers so once you have found that the drum and cymbal both sound on second 41, the bell will also sound then as it is an odd number.

25–28 A straight line has 180° so the missing angle can be found by subtracting the given angle from 180°.
25 **142** 180° − 38° = 142°
26 **85** 180° − 95° = 85°
27 **65** 180° − 115° = 65°
28 **135** 180° − 45° = 135°

29–31 **E = 30°, F = 80°, G = 100°** The angles in a triangle add up to 180°, so Angle E can be found by subtracting the other two angles from 180° (180° − 70° − 80° = 30°). To find angle G, look at the quadrilateral it is part of. Angles in a quadrilateral add up to 360°. Subtract the 3 known angles from 360°. 110 + 70 + 80 = 260; 360 − 260 = 100. Angles G and F form a straight line so, to find angle F, subtract 100 from 180.

32 **140** See Focus test 8, Q1. Find the area of the whole rectangle (12 m × 15 m = 180 m²) and the area of the smaller rectangle (5 m × 8 = 40 m²). Then subtract the area of the smaller rectangle from the area of the whole rectangle to find the area of the shaded section (180 m² − 140 m² = 140 m²).

33 **80** See Focus test 8, Q1. Find the perimeter of the shaded outside (12 m + 15 m + 12 m + 15 m = 54 m) and the perimeter of the inner rectangle (5 m + 8 m + 5 m + 8 m = 26 m), then add them together to find the total perimeter (54 m + 26 m = 80 m).

34 **37 days** The two oldest creatures are Crunch and Whizz. Crunch is born on 8 December and there are 31 days in December, so 31 − 8 = 23 days to the end of the year. Whizz is born on 14 January, so 23 days + 14 days = 37 days.

35 **415 cm** First convert all the heights into cm (1.10 m × 100 = 110 cm; 1.60 m × 100 = 160 cm; 1.45 m × 100 = 145 cm). Then add them together to find the combined height in centimetres (110 cm + 160 cm + 145 cm = 415 cm).

36 **23 450 g** First find the weights of the heaviest and lightest creatures and convert them into grams (22.85 × 1000 = 22 850 g; 46.3 × 1000 = 46 300 g). Then subtract the lightest from the heaviest (46 300 g − 22 850 g = 23 450 g).

37 **no** The combined weight is 22.85 kg + 46.3 kg + 38.92 kg = 108.07 kg.

38 **2.4 m** 50% of Zoom's height would be 0.8 m (1.6 m ÷ 2). Add this amount to his original height: 1.6 m + 0.8 m = 2.4 m.

39–42 **(3, 0), (0, 7), (7, 4), (4, 3)**

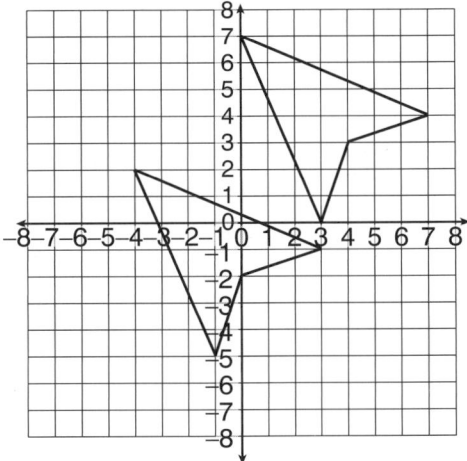

43 **240** Locate April from the months on the x-axis. Move upwards from this point until it touches the solid black line, which represents the girls' birthdays. Move to the left from this point to read off the number of births.

44 **June** Locate the point where the solid black line and the dotted black line are together and move down to find the month.

45 **100** Locate September and subtract the number of girls from the number of boys (320 − 220 = 100).

46 **August** Locate the month where the gap between the girls and the boys is biggest.

47 **poor chance** The chance of picking a 1 is not impossible as there is a 1 in the cards, but there are 8 more chances of picking a number that is 2 or higher, so this is a poor chance.

48 **good chance** There are 5 odd numbers (1, 3, 5, 7, 9) and 4 even numbers (2, 4, 6, 8) so the chance of picking an odd number is more than even, but it is not certain as there are even numbers. This makes it a good chance.

49 **impossible** There are no zeros available, so it is impossible to pick one.

50 **5** See Focus test 12, Q2. The cards in order are: 1, 2, 3, 4, **5**, 6, 7, 8, 9.

Mixed Paper 7 (pages 46–50)

1–2 **670 000, 675 000** When rounding a number to the nearest 10 000, look at the number in the thousands column. If it is 4 or below, leave the number in the ten thousands column unchanged. If it is 5 or above, raise the number in the ten thousands column by 1. For rounding a number to the nearest 1000, see Focus test 1, Q12.

3–4 **700 000, 691 100** When rounding a number to the nearest 100 000, look at the number in the ten thousand columns. If it is 4 or below, leave the number in the hundred thousands column unchanged. If it is 5 or above, raise the number in the hundred thousands column by 1. When rounding a number to the nearest 100, look at the number in the tens column. If it is 4 or below, leave the number in the hundreds column unchanged. If it is 5 or above, raise the number in the hundreds column by 1.

5–6 **Tunnel of Terror, Dodgem Boats** The most popular ride was the Rocky Roller Coaster, with 897 529 people. To find the pair of rides that equal this, look at the number on the far left to make sure the pair of numbers is not larger than 8. 6 + 3 and 6 + 6 are too big, so 3 + 5 seems to be the logical pair. Work out the sum to check your answer (591 643 + 305 886 = 897 529).

7–8 **3 160 707, 3 160 710** Use column addition to add the total number of people who went on the rides.

	8	9	7	5	2	9
	6	7	4	5	8	6
+	5	9	1	6	4	3
	3	0	5	8	8	6
	6	9	1	0	6	3
3	1	6	0	7	0	7
		3	2	2	3	2
3	1	6	0	7	0	7

To round a number to the nearest 10, look at the number in the ones column. If it is 4 or below, leave the number in the tens column unchanged. If it is 5 or above, raise the number in the tens column by 1. 3 160 707 rounded to the nearest 10 is 3 160 710.

9–11

−	12.376	21.2
5.94	**6.436**	15.26
8.683	**3.693**	**12.517**

To find 6.436, subtract 5.94 from 12.376. Subtract 8.683 from 12.376 to find 3.693, then subtract 8.683 from 21.2 to find 12.517.

12 **3, 5, 11** Make a list of the prime numbers below 15: 2, 3, 5, 7, 11 and 13. The end digit is a 5, so you will need to use the 5. Test combinations to find the other two numbers. Use a trial and improvement method to find the correct combination: if you get a total that is too big, choose a smaller number and vice versa.

13 **45** A right-angled triangle has one 90° angle and an isosceles triangle has two angles the same. The three angles of a triangle total 180°, so subtract the right angle and then divide the result by two to find the missing angle (180° − 90° = 90°; 90° ÷ 2 = 45°).

14–15 **96, 128** Divide each number by 8 and see which gives a whole number as the result.

16–17 **(2, 46)** The last digit of 92 is 2, making it an even number, so it must have 2 as a factor. Use division to find the other half of the factor pair (92 ÷ 2 = 46).

18 **25%** The whole grid has 12 squares and 3 of them are light grey, so $\frac{3}{12}$ are light grey. To turn this into a percentage, use equivalent fractions to make the denominator 100. The numerator is now a percentage ($\frac{3}{12} = \frac{1}{4} = \frac{25}{100} = 25\%$).

19 $\frac{1}{3}$ The whole grid has 12 squares and 4 of them are dark grey, so $\frac{4}{12}$ are dark grey. This is equivalent to $\frac{1}{3}$.

20 **<** Turn the fraction into a decimal by changing the fifths into tenths $2\frac{3}{5} = 2\frac{6}{10}$. Then change $\frac{6}{10}$ into a decimal to give 2.6 and compare to 2.35.

21 **60%** If 18 of the 30 children are girls, this gives $\frac{18}{30}$. To convert this fraction into a percentage, first use an equivalent fraction to make the denominator 100. The numerator is now a percentage ($\frac{18}{30} = \frac{6}{10} = \frac{60}{100} = 60\%$).

22–25 See Focus test 6, Q1.

22 **d** From 40 to 50 is +10; from 50 to 70 is +20; from 70 to 100 is +30. The pattern is that the number added goes up by 10 each time, so 100 + 40 = 140.

23–24 **49, 81** In this sequence the numbers are square numbers from 4^2 to 11^2.

25 **21** The sequence is +1, +2, +3, +4, +5, so 15 + 6 = 21.

26–29

	1 or more rectangular faces	No rectangular faces
1 or more triangular faces	D	C
No triangular faces	A	B

The triangular prism (D) has 3 rectangular faces and 2 triangular faces. The cuboid (A) has 6 rectangular faces but no triangular faces. The tetrahedron (C) has no rectangular faces but 4 triangular faces. The cylinder (B) has no triangular faces and no rectangular faces.

30 **96** See Focus test 8, Q1. 12 m × 8 m = 96 m²

31 **354** See Focus test 8, Q10. 30 m × 15 m = 450 m²; 450 m² − 96 m² = 354 m²

32 **60** First, find the perimeter (30 + 15 + 30 + 15 = 90). Then divide the perimeter by 1.5 m to find the number of panels needed (90 ÷ 1.5 m = 60).

33 As area is length × width, find the factor pairs of 64 (1 × 64, 2 × 32, 4 × 16, 8 × 8). One long side and one short side make up half the perimeter, which is 20 (40 ÷ 2 = 20). Check the factor pairs to find the one that adds up to 20.

34 **90 mm** Each brick is 4.5 cm long, so two bricks are 9 cm long.

35 **22.5** 4.5 cm × 5 = 22.5 cm

36 **8** Subtract the combined weight of Parcels B and C from 14 kg (15 kg − 7 kg = 8 kg).

37 **4** A is twice the weight of B, so 8 kg ÷ 2 = 4 kg.

38 **3** B + C = 7 kg and B weighs 4 kg, so 7 kg − 4 kg = 3 kg.

39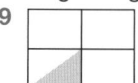

The triangle is rotated clockwise by 90° each time.

40 **(6, 7)** The missing coordinate has the same x-axis position as the bottom right-hand corner, which is 6. The missing coordinate has the same y-axis position as the top left-hand corner, which is 7.

41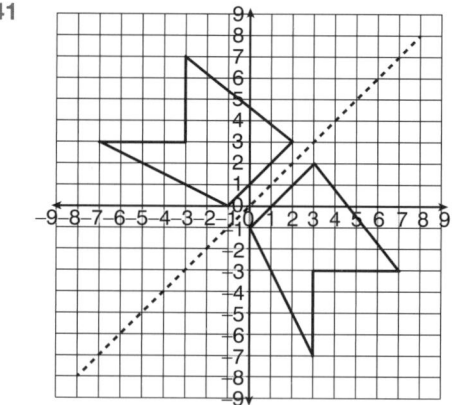

42 **(3, −3)** Work through the coordinates to find the pair that are not on the mirror line.

43–46 The whole pie chart represents £4 and is divided into 8 equal sections. Each section is 50p (£4 ÷ 8 = 50p).

43 **£2.50** The amount that Kate saved is a quarter which is £10 ÷ 4 = £2.50.

44 **£3.75** The boat ride takes up 3 sections, which is £3.75 (3 × £1.25).

45 **£1.25** Sweets take up 1 section, which is £1.25.
46 **£7.50** Kate saved £2.50 out of a total of £10, so subtract this to find the total money spent (£10 − £2.50 = £7.50).
47 **7** See Focus test 12, Q1. Here, one of the numbers is missing ((9 + ?) ÷ 2 = 8). Work backwards to find it (8 × 2 = 16; 16 − 9 = 7).
48 **16** 512 ÷ 32 = 16
49 **0.6** Probability is always out of 1, so 1.0 − 0.4 = 0.6.
50 **50%** There are an equal number of chances for a coin to land on heads or on tails, and equal chance can be expressed as 1 in 2, $\frac{1}{2}$, 0.50 or 50%.

Mixed Paper 8 (pages 50–55)

1–4 **4.602 < 4.604 < 6.024 < 6.246** See Focus test 1, Q11.

T	U	•	t	h	th
	6	•	0	2	4
	4	•	6	0	2
	4	•	6	0	4
	6	•	2	4	6

5–7 **A = 2, B = 4, C = 6** Look at the ones column and find the 2 by working out what even numbers can be added to make 2. As they are all B, it is the same number and the 2 must represent 12. This means B must be 4 (12 ÷ 3 = 4) and 1 is carried over. Subtract this 1 from the 3 in the answers to the tens column to see that A + 4 + C = 12 or 22. The hundreds column has C + C + 4 = 17 and as this is an odd number, 1 must have been carried over. Subtract this to find C + C + 4 = 16, so C must be 6 (6 + 6 + 4 + 1 = 17). Finally, return to the tens column. A + 4 + 6 = 12, so A must be 2.
8 **612** Convert the words to digits, then multiply both numbers by 10 to find a whole number as the divisor (1836 ÷ 3 = 612).
9–10 **1.8 kg, 2.8 kg** Subtract 3.5 kg from the total weight to find the combined weight of the two missing parcels (8.1 kg − 3.5 kg = 4.6 kg). As there is a difference of 1 kg between the missing two parcels, divide the weight in half and then add 0.5 kg to one weight and remove 0.5 kg from the other to give a difference of 1 kg (4.6 kg ÷ 2 = 2.3 kg; 2.3 kg + 0.5 kg = 2.8 kg; 2.3 kg − 0.5 kg = 1.8 kg).
11 **69** Find the number in the eight times table that falls between 60 and 70 and then add 5 to it (8 × 8 = 64; 64 + 5 = 69).
12 **6** Divide 78 eggs into 12 boxes and round down (78 ÷ 12 = 6 r 6, making 6 complete boxes).
13 **63** Solve this by reversing the operations and working backwards (450 ÷ 50 = 9; 9 × 7 = 63).
14 **12** Divide 30 kg by 2.5 kg. To make this easier, work in whole numbers by multiplying both numbers by 10 (300 kg ÷ 25 kg = 12).
15 **False** Any odd number multiplied by an even number has an even number answer, such as 9 × 4 = 36 or 9 × 8 = 72.
16 **True** The digits of every multiple of 9 can be divided exactly by 9. For example, 9 × 4 = 36 and 3 + 6 = 9 and 1 × 9 = 9, or 9 × 8 = 72 and 7 + 2 = 9 and 1 × 9 = 9.
17 **False** The factors of 30 are 1 × 30, 2 × 15, 3 × 10, 5 × 6. That is a total of 8 factors.
18 **True** The factors of a square number will always be odd because one factor pair is made up of the same number repeated, for example 36 is 6 × 6, which is 1 factor.
19–20 **0.8, $\frac{3}{5}$** To find the numbers that are more than $\frac{1}{2}$, find the decimal and percentage equivalents to $\frac{1}{2}$ and compare whether a card is higher than these equivalents. $\frac{1}{2}$ = 0.5 = 50%, so 8% is less than 50%; $\frac{3}{8}$ is less than $\frac{4}{8}$, which is an equivalent of $\frac{1}{2}$; 0.8 is more than 0.5; 0.35 is less than 0.5; $\frac{3}{5} = \frac{30}{50}$, which is more than $\frac{25}{50} = \frac{1}{2}$; 38% is less than 50%.
21 **£96** Use equivalent fractions to add the three fractions together $\left(\frac{3}{8} = \frac{15}{40}, \frac{2}{5} = \frac{16}{40}, \frac{1}{10} = \frac{4}{40}; \frac{15}{40} + \frac{16}{40} + \frac{4}{40} = \frac{35}{40}\right)$. This is the amount that Abinaath has spent, so he has $\frac{5}{40}$ of his money remaining, which is equivalent to $\frac{1}{8}$. This is equal to £12, so multiply £12 × 8 = £96.
22–24 Add up the percentages and take this away from 100% to find what percentage is spent on dried fruit (33% + 15% + 28% = 76%; 100% − 76% = 24%). Divide £48 by this percentage to find out how much 1% is in money (£48 ÷ 24 = £2). Now multiply this amount by the percentages of each item to find the amount of money spent.
22 **£66** If 1% = £2, then £2 × 33 = £66 spent on flour.
23 **£56** £2 × 28 = £56 spent on butter
24 **£30** £2 × 15 = £30 spent on sugar
25–26 **7.2, 194.4** To find each number, multiply the previous number in the sequence by 3 (3 × 2.4 = 7.2), (3 × 64.8 = 194.4).
27–28 **1710, 3210** See Focus test 6, Q1. From 2010 to 2310 is +300 and from 2310 to 2610 is also +300, so the rule is to add 300 each time. 2910 + 300 = 3210 and 2010 − 300 = 1710

29 **45°** A right-angle is 90°, so when it is divided in half it leaves 2 angles of 45° each.
30 **Line CD** Parallel lines face in the same direction, are always the same distance apart and never meet.
31 **isosceles** or **right-angled** An isosceles triangle has two sides the same. A right-angled triangle has one angle which is 90°. Triangle ABD is both an isosceles and a right-angled triangle, so either answer is correct.
32 **never** A cube has 6 square faces. A cuboid has rectangular faces.
33 **13** Count all of the whole squares first and then match the half squares and add them to the total.
34 **2** The area of the lawn is 7.5 m × 4 m = 30 m². The Seed and Feed treats 15 m², so 30 m² ÷ 15 m² = 2 packs.
35 **105** Divide the shape into 1 long rectangle and 2 shorter rectangles. Work out the area for each, then add the total together. A = 3 cm × (8 + 3 + 8) = 3 cm × 19 cm = 57 cm², B = 3 cm × 8 cm = 24 cm²; C = 3 cm × 8 cm = 24 cm². Total area = 24 cm² + 24 cm² + 57 cm² = 105 cm²

36 **76 cm** See Focus test 8, Q1. There are 4 ends of the rectangles, so 4 × 3 cm = 12 cm. There are 8 sides of the rectangles, so 8 × 8 cm = 64 cm. Add these together to find the total perimeter (12 cm + 64 cm = 76 cm).
37 **500** There are 10 increments in each litre, so each small increment is worth 100 ml (1000 ml ÷ 10 = 100 ml). Jug A has 2300 ml and Jug B has 1800, so subtract to find the difference (2300 ml – 1800 ml = 500 ml).
38 **900** Find the amount of both jugs added together (2300 ml + 1800 ml = 4100 ml). Multiply 5 litres by 1000 to find the equivalent in ml (5 × 1000 = 5000 ml). Finally, subtract the amount in the jugs from the size of the bowl (5000 ml – 4100 ml = 900 ml).
39–40 **=, <** See Focus test 9, Q12. 40.5 cm × 10 = 405 mm = 405 mm; 180 g ÷ 1000 = 0.18 kg < 1.8 kg

41–42 **(3, –1), (4, 2), (3, 5)**

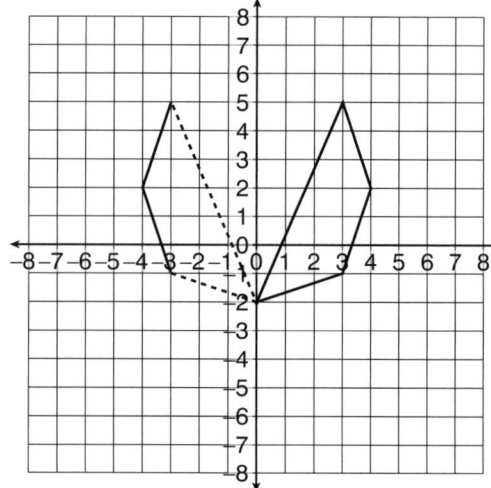

43 **March** Locate 10 degrees on the y-axis and follow this to the right until it meets the temperature line. Follow this point down to read the months on the x-axis.
44 **13°C** Locate April on the x-axis and follow this up until it meets the temperature line. Follow this point left to read the temperature on the y-axis.
45 **May** Locate September on the x-axis. Follow this up until it meets the temperature line. Follow this point to the left and right to locate another month that shares the same temperature.
46 **16°C** Locate the lowest point of the temperature line and note the temperature on the y-axis. Next, locate the highest point of the temperature line and note the temperature on the y-axis. Subtract the lowest temperature from the highest (21°C – 5°C = 16°C).
47–49 See Focus test 12, Q1.
47 **20°C** 19°C + 21°C + 20°C = 60°C; 60°C ÷ 3 = 20°C
48 **6°C** 5°C + 5°C + 8°C = 18°C; 18°C ÷ 3 = 6°C
49 **12.75°C** 5°C + 8°C + 10°C + 13°C + 16°C + 19°C + 21°C + 20°C + 16°C + 11°C + 9°C + 5°C = 153°C; 153°C ÷ 12 = 12.75°C
50 **12°C** See Focus test 12, Q2. The temperatures in order are: 5°C, 5°C, 8°C, 9°C, 10°C, **11°C, 13°C**, 16°C, 16°C, 19°C, 20°C, 21°C. If there are two numbers in the middle, add them together and divide by 2 to find the median (11°C + 13°C = 24°C; 24°C ÷ 2 = 12°C).

45 How many jumpers were sold in total? _____

46 Is the following statement true or false? _____

"Hats were the only item that sold more for men than women."

These are Tom's scores in a daily spelling test over one week.
Monday→14   Tuesday→15   Wednesday→18   Thursday→14   Friday→19

47 What is Tom's mean score? _____

48 What is Tom's median score? _____

49 What is Tom's mode score? _____

50 What is the range of his scores? _____

Now go to the Progress Chart to record your score!   Total

Mixed paper 3

1–5 These are the average depths of the deepest oceans and seas in the world.

Write each depth to the nearest 1000 m.

Ocean/Sea	Average depth (metres)	Rounded to nearest 1000 m
Atlantic Ocean	3926	_____
Caribbean Sea	2647	_____
Pacific Ocean	4028	_____
Indian Ocean	3963	_____
South China Sea	1652	_____

6 Find the sum of 4.3, 16.792, 6 and 0.95. _____

7 What are the numbers A and B?

A = _____   B = _____

A and B are two different decimal numbers. A is 3.6 greater than B.
A + B = 12.42

8 The letters A, B and C stand for three consecutive numbers from 1–9. Using the grid below, work out which number each letter represents.

	A	B	C
+	B	A	A
1	2	2	2

A = ____ B = ____ C = ____

9 Use the three bills below to work out the cost of 1 drink, 1 sandwich and 1 cake.

Table 1	Table 2	Table 3
2 drinks	2 drinks	4 drinks
2 sandwiches	2 sandwiches	2 sandwiches
1 cake	2 cakes	4 cakes
£12.30	£13.50	£19.50

1 drink = ____   1 sandwich = ____   1 cake = ____

10–13 This is a 'divide by 30 machine'. Write the missing numbers in the chart.

IN → ÷ 30 → OUT

IN	150	____	360	450	____
OUT	____	8	____	15	20

14–15 Circle the two numbers that are prime numbers.

29   39   49   59   69

16 Write a multiple of 8 that would make this number sentence true.

110 < ____ < 120

17 Write a factor of 60 that would make this number sentence true.

15 > ____ > 10

18 Write these numbers in order, starting with the smallest.

$\frac{16}{20}$ 38%   0.76 $\frac{12}{40}$ 72%   0.49

____ ____ ____ ____ ____ ____

Smallest →

19 The following three books have been reduced by 18% in the shop. What is their new sale price?

Book 1	Book 2	Book 3
£20.00	£24.00	£16.00
_____	_____	_____

Class 1 has 32 children in it. On Monday $\frac{3}{16}$ of the children were absent and half this number were absent on Tuesday. The rest of the week, nobody was absent.

Class 2 has 30 children in it. On Monday 10% of the children were absent and double this number were absent on Tuesday. The rest of the week, nobody was absent.

20 How many children were absent from classes 1 and 2 on Tuesday?
_____

21 What was the total number of children in school from classes 1 and 2 for the full week? _____

22 What is the missing number in this sequence? Circle the correct answer.

41   50   60   71   ____   96

a 85   **b** 83   **c** 81   **d** 87

23 What is the rule or pattern for this sequence? Circle the correct answer.

0   2.5   5   7.5   10

a double the number   **b** halve the number   **c** add 0.5   **d** add 2.5

24 Write the missing numbers in this sequence.

59.6   49.1   38.6   ____   17.6   7.1   ____

25 Write the missing mixed number fraction in this sequence.

____ $5\frac{4}{5}$ $4\frac{7}{10}$ $3\frac{3}{5}$ $2\frac{1}{2}$ $1\frac{2}{5}$

26 Name the shape this net will make when it is folded. _____

27 Measure this angle carefully with a protractor. _____ °

28 Circle the shape that is a regular polygon.

A   B   C   D   E   F

29–30 Draw two lines of symmetry on this shape.

Calculate the perimeter of these squares.

31 Area = 49 cm²   Perimeter = _____ cm

32 Area = 9 cm²   Perimeter = _____ cm

33–34 What are the perimeter and area of a swimming pool that is seven metres wide and twelve metres long?

Perimeter = _____ m   Area = _____ m²

Write the amount shown in each jug in millilitres.

35 _____ ml

36 _____ ml

37 What is the difference between the amount of liquid in these two jugs? _____ ml

38 The liquid in these two jugs is poured into an empty bucket. How much liquid is in the bucket? _____ litres

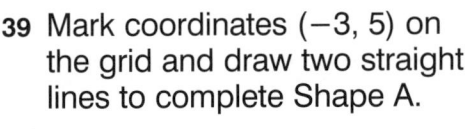

39 Mark coordinates (−3, 5) on the grid and draw two straight lines to complete Shape A.

40 Mark coordinates (4, 0) on the grid and draw two straight lines to complete Shape B.

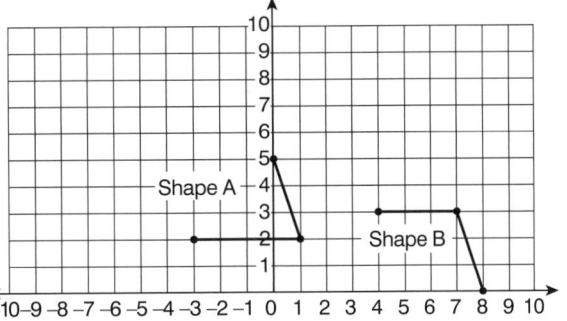

41 Circle the correct transformation of Shape A to Shape B.

Translation   Rotation   Reflection

42 Circle the coordinates that match one of the vertices of Shape A.

(2, 1)   (3, 3)   (−3, 0)   (0, 5)   (2, −3)

43 How many children are over 1.6 m in height? _____

44 Which range of heights is the mode?

Circle the correct range.

130 cm or under   131 cm–140 cm

141 cm–150 cm   151 cm–160 cm

161 cm or over

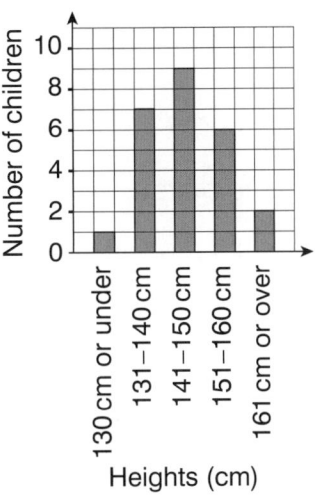

Heights of children in Class H (to the nearest cm)

45 How many children are 140 cm or less in height? _____

46 How many children are there in total in Class H? _____

There are 4 red, 2 green and 6 yellow balloons. One of the balloons bursts.

```
0                                              1
|----------|----------|----------|----------|
impossible  unlikely  even chance  likely   certain
```

47 What is the chance that the burst balloon was yellow? _____

48 What is the chance that the burst balloon was red? _____

49 What is the chance that the burst balloon was **not** green?
_____

50 What is the chance that the burst balloon was blue? _____

Now go to the Progress Chart to record your score! Total ◯ 50

Mixed paper 4

1–4 Write the numbers at each position on this number line.

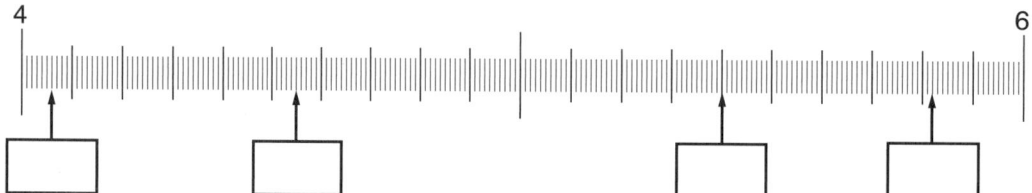

Shopping receipt A has these amounts: 76p, £1.38, 23p, £4.99, £10.12, 14p.
Shopping receipt B has these amounts: £2.99, £13.94, £3.50, £1.95, 56p, 82p.

5 What is the difference in cost between shopping receipt A and shopping receipt B? _____

6 How much change will there be if shopping receipts A and B are paid for with 2 £20 notes and 1 £10 note? _____

This table shows the distance of flights from London to Rome and New York.

7 What is the distance of a **return** flight from London to Rome?
_____ km

	Rome	New York
London	1459 km	5557 km

8 How much further from London is New York than Rome?
_____ km

9 0.38 × 1.2 = _____

10 43.21 × 0.8 = _____

11 What is the smallest number that can be added to 450 to make it exactly divisible by 8? _____

12 In a survey of how children travelled to school, one third of the 357 children walked. How many children walked to school?
_____

13–14 Circle the two numbers that are a multiple of 7.

27   39   44   56   68   73   85   91

15–16 Write the missing pair of factors for 54.

(1, 54)   (2, 27)   (____, ____)   (6, 9)

Circle the mixed number with the same value as the improper fraction.

17 $\frac{7}{2}$ $7\frac{1}{2}$ $3\frac{1}{7}$ $2\frac{1}{3}$ $3\frac{1}{2}$ $1\frac{2}{7}$

18 $\frac{12}{5}$ $2\frac{2}{5}$ $1\frac{2}{5}$ $6\frac{1}{5}$ $2\frac{2}{10}$ $2\frac{1}{5}$

Here is the start of a number sequence.

3   7   11   15   19   23

19 Which of these numbers is NOT a prime number? _____

20 If the sequence continued, what would be the largest number that is less than 50? _____

21 What is the first term of this number sequence?

____   1.0101   10.101   101.01   1010.1   10 101

Look at these patterns.

22 What is the rule for this sequence? _____

23 How many dots will be in a pattern that has 8 dots on the bottom row? _____

24 How many rows will there be if there is a total of 78 dots? _____

25 Calculate the size of angle *x* on this isosceles triangle. _____°

26 Complete this statement with **always**, **sometimes** or **never**.

Triangles are _____ symmetrical.

27 Measure this angle carefully with a protractor.

_____ °

Look at the floor plan below. Tiles are 50 cm square and need to cover the floor.

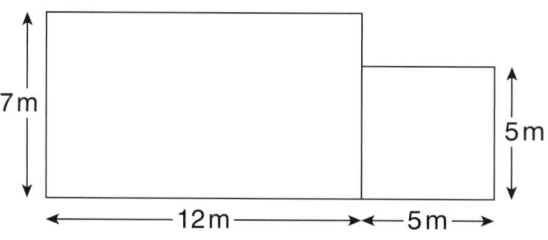

28 What is the total area of the floor? _____

29 How many tiles are needed to cover the whole floor? _____

30 Which has the larger area, Room A or Room B? Room _____

31 Which has the longer perimeter? Underline the statement that is true.

    Room A has the longer perimeter.

    Room B has the longer perimeter.

    The perimeters of Room A and Room B are the same length.

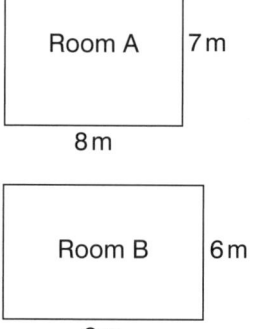

32–34 Write this set of measures in order, starting with the smallest.

    1.6 km   3000 mm   14.5 m   146 cm   0.32 km   450 000 mm

____ ____ ____ ____ ____ ____

Smallest →

35 A bucket holds 12 litres of water. A cup holds 300 ml of water. A ladle holds 100 ml of water. If Ali fills 20 cups and 40 ladles of water from a bucket full of water, how much water will be left in the bucket, in litres? _____

36–39 Plot these coordinates and join them in order to make a quadrilateral. Label each point with a letter.
Draw a line from point D to point A.

A (1, 3)   B (−2, 6)
C (−5, 3)   D (−2, −5)

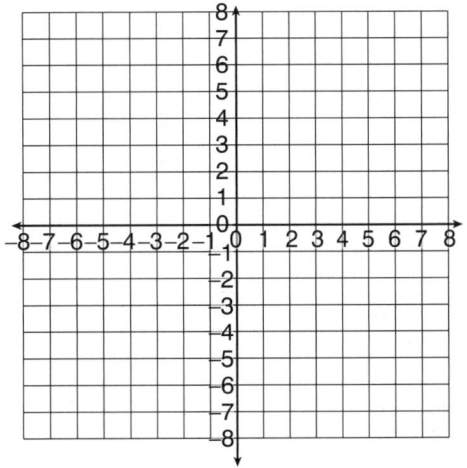

40 What is the name of this quadrilateral? _____

41 How many lines of symmetry are there on this shape? _____

42 Is the angle at (−2, −5) on this shape reflex, obtuse, acute or a right angle? _____

Look at this conversion chart.

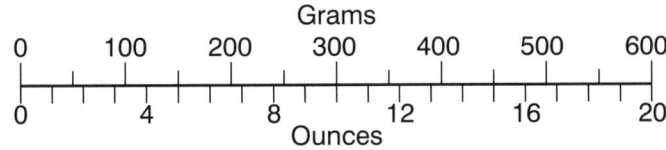

43 Approximately how many grams are there in 20 ounces? _____

44 Approximately how many ounces are there in 450 grams? _____

45–46 An old recipe for biscuits lists the amount of each ingredient in ounces. Use the chart to convert each amount to grams.

Butter   5 ounces → _____ grams

Flour   10 ounces → _____ grams

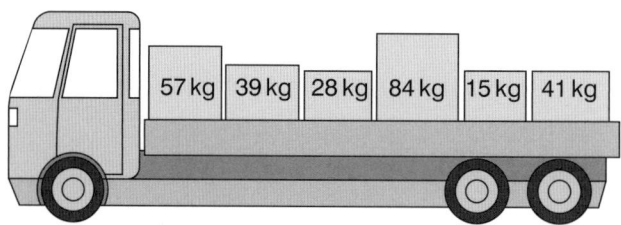

47 What is the mean weight of the boxes on this lorry? _____

48 What is the median weight of the boxes on this lorry? _____

49–50 Another box weighing 30 kg is placed on the lorry.

What is the mean weight now? _____

What is the median weight now? _____

Now go to the Progress Chart to record your score!   Total   50

Mixed paper 5

Answer the following calculations:

1 0.06 × 100 = _____

2 23.1 × 100 = _____

3 1806 ÷ 100 = _____

4 72 ÷ 100 = _____

In the Mahalangur Himalaya mountain range, Mount Everest is 9000 m, rounded to the nearest 1000 m. Mount Makalu is 8500 m, rounded to the nearest 100 m. Mount Khartaphu is 7000 m rounded to the nearest 1000 m and 7200 m rounded to the nearest 100 m.

5 What are the minimum and maximum possible heights of Mount Everest from this information? _____, _____

6 What are the minimum and maximum possible heights of Mount Makalu from this information? _____, _____

7 What are the minimum and maximum possible heights of Mount Khartaphu from this information? _____, _____

8–9 Complete the following pyramid. Each pair of numbers on the bottom row are multiplied together to form the number on the row above.

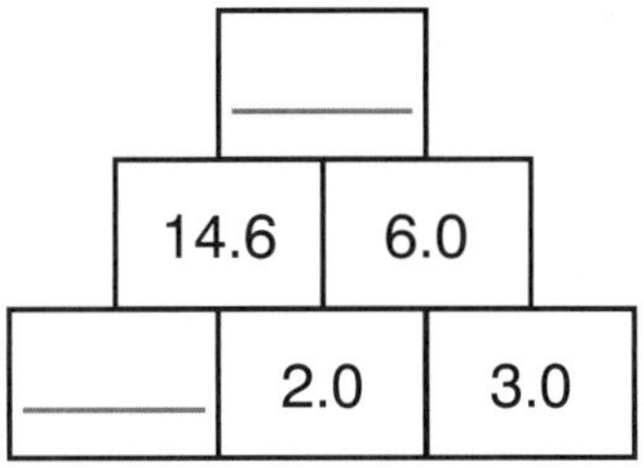

	14.6	6.0
___	2.0	3.0

10 Apples cost £1.50 per kilogram. How many kilograms of apples can be bought for £12? _____ kg

11–12 Circle two numbers which, when multiplied together, have the answer closest to 70.

        8   17   9   23   6   3

13 I am thinking of a number. If I multiply it by 6 and divide it by 42 the answer is 18. What is my number? _____

14 $h^3 = 64$. What is the value of h? _____

15 What is the next prime number after 13? _____

16–17 Write the missing factors of 57 in order.

        57 → 1 _____ _____ 57

On a train there are 45 boys. Girls make up 40% of the train. $\frac{1}{5}$ of the passengers are women and $\frac{3}{10}$ are men.

18 How many people are on the train? _____

19 How many girls are on the train? _____

20 How many women are on the train? _____

21 How many men are on the train? _____

Continue these patterns for two more numbers.

22–23   56   65   74   83   ____   ____

24–25   391   388   385   382   ____   ____

Look at these shapes and answer the questions.

A

B
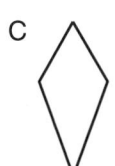
C
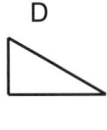
D
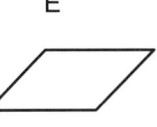
E

26 How many shapes are quadrilaterals? _____

27 How many shapes have no lines of symmetry? _____

28 How many shapes have a reflex angle inside? _____

29 How many shapes have obtuse angles inside? _____

30 The area of a square is 100 cm². What is the length of one side of this square? _____ cm

31–32 Calculate the area and perimeter of this rectangle.

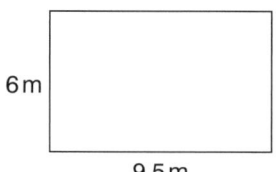

Area = _____ m²

Perimeter = _____ m

33 A football pitch is 95 m by 65 m. A white line is marked out around the whole perimeter of the pitch. How long is the white line? _____ m

34–35 Look at the map and complete this bus timetable.

Vale Bus Station	11:50
Welbourn Church	_____
Yarley School	12:39
Zennor Bridge	_____

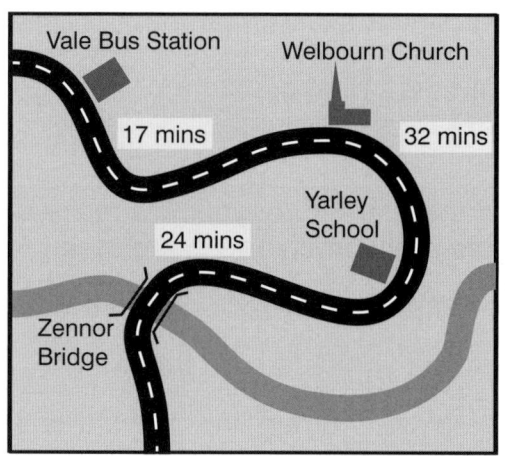

36 How long in total was the bus journey from Vale Bus Station to Zennor Bridge? ____ hour ____ minutes

37 The bus was 4 minutes early at Yarley School. What time did the bus arrive at Yarley School? _____

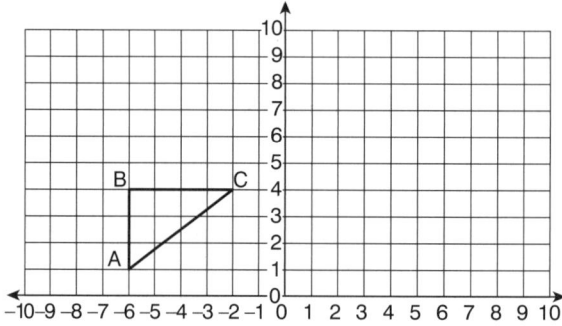

38–39 Write the missing coordinates for this triangle.

A →(____, ____)   B →(____, ____)   C → (−2, 4)

40 Circle the coordinates that can be found inside this triangle.

(−1, 2)   (−4, 6)   (3, −4)   (−5, 3)   (2, −2)

41 The triangle is rotated clockwise around point (−2, 4) so that vertex A is at (−5, 8). Where is the new position of vertex B? (____, ____)

The Venn diagram shows the food children in a class had in their lunch boxes after they had eaten their sandwiches.

42 How many children had fruit and cake but no yoghurt? _____

43 How many children only had a piece of fruit? _____

44 How many children had a yoghurt, fruit and cake in their box? _____

45 How many children had a yoghurt in their lunch box? _____

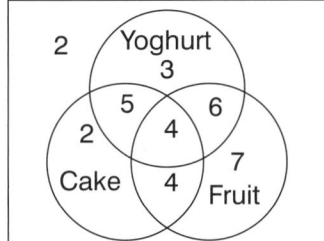

46

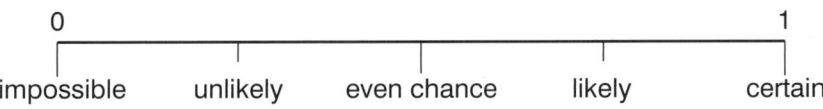

Circle the chance of rolling an even number on a 1–6 dice.

| 35 cm | 25 cm | 15 cm | 25 cm | 35 cm | 35 cm | 15 cm | 25 cm | 35 cm |

47 What is the mode of these lengths? _____

48 What is the median of these lengths? _____

49 What is the range of these lengths? _____

50 What is the mean of these four numbers?   19   24   27   12

_____

Now go to the Progress Chart to record your score!   Total   50

Mixed paper 6

1–2 Circle the smallest number and underline the largest number.

36.06   36.604   34.064   36.46   34.6

3–4 The secret code to unlock a padlock has 4 digits made from 2 double-digit numbers. The first double digit is between 10 and 15. The second double digit is the first double digit multiplied by 3. The secret code has NO digits of the same value. What is the code? _____

5 How much more will it cost to buy the table than a chair? £_____

6 How much would it cost to buy a table and two chairs? £_____

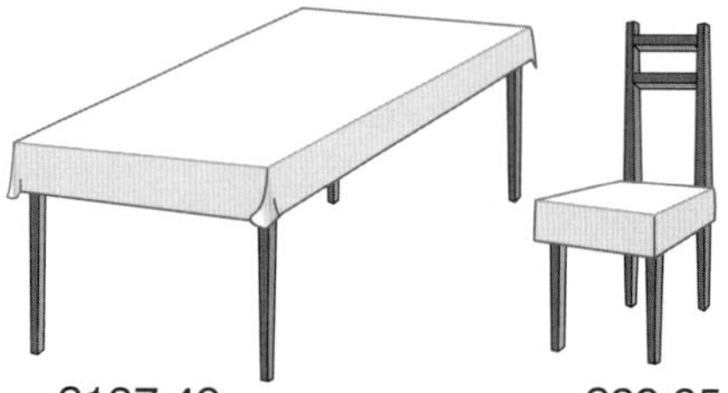

7 Mr and Mrs Jays have £95. How much more do they need to buy the table? £_____

£137.49   £89.95

8 Mr and Mrs Jays decide to buy one chair. How much money will they have left from £95 if they buy one chair? £_____

9 The area of a rectangle is 234 cm². The shorter side is 9 cm. What is the length of the longer side? _____ cm

10 Ryan is 7 and his mother is six times older than he is. His grandfather is twice as old as his mother. How old is Ryan's grandfather? _____ years

11 A school bus travels 40 km a day. The bus takes children to school on 5 days every week. There are 12 weeks in a term and 3 terms in a year. How far does the school bus travel in a year? _____

12 340 sandwiches are made for a wedding party, so that there are 4 sandwiches for each person. There will also be enough tomatoes for everyone to have 3 tomatoes each. How many tomatoes will be needed in total? _____

13–16 Write these numbers in the correct part of this Carroll diagram.

24   36   48   60

	A factor of 72	Not a factor of 72
A multiple of 8	_____	_____
Not a multiple of 8	_____	_____

42

17–18 Which two of these are equivalent to 20%? Circle the correct answers.

0.2 $\frac{2}{5}$ 0.5   0.02 $\frac{1}{5}$

19–20 Answer these.

$\frac{3}{8} + \frac{1}{2} = \frac{\Box}{\Box}$ $\frac{7}{10} - \frac{1}{5} = \frac{\Box}{\Box}$

21 Look at this pattern made from wooden sticks.

   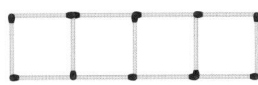

How many sticks are required to make a 15 square pattern?

_____

Write the missing number in each sequence.

22 10   8.8   _____   6.4   5.2

23 60   210   360   _____   660

24 A music program plays a sequence in which a drum sounds every 4 seconds, a cymbal sounds every 5 seconds and a bell sounds every 2 seconds. They all make a noise together at 1 second. At what second will they next all make a noise together? _____

Calculate the missing angles. Do not use a protractor.

25

Angle A = _____°

26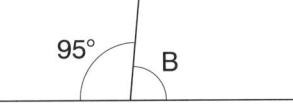

Angle B = _____°

27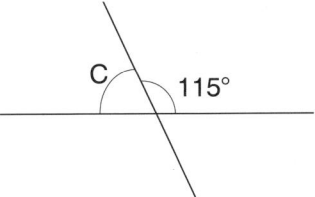

Angle C = _____°

28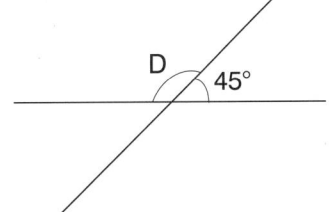

Angle D = _____°

29–31 Angle E = ____°

Angle F = ____°

Angle G = ____°

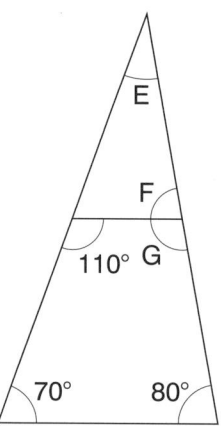

Calculate the area and total perimeter of this shaded shape.

32 Area = ____ m²

33 Perimeter = ____ m

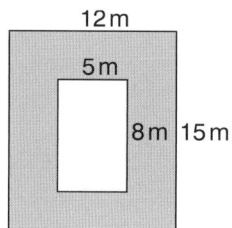

Look at the three creatures below and the table of details about them.

Whizz   Zoom   Crunch

	Whizz	**Zoom**	**Crunch**
Weight	22.85 kg	46.3 kg	38.92 kg
Height	1.10 m	1.60 m	1.45 m
Date of Birth	14/01/2010	26/02/2011	8/12/2009

34 What is the difference in age between the two oldest creatures in days? _____

35 What is the combined height of all three creatures in centimetres? _____

36 What is the difference in weight between the lightest and heaviest creatures in grams? _____

37 A ride at the fair has a maximum weight of 108 kg in one compartment. Will all three creatures be able to fit into one compartment?

_____

38 If Zoom grows in height by 50% in the next year, how tall will he be?

_____

39–42 Translate this shape so that it is 4 squares right and 5 squares up. Write the coordinates of each vertex of this translated shape.

(____, ____) (____, ____)

(____, ____) (____, ____)

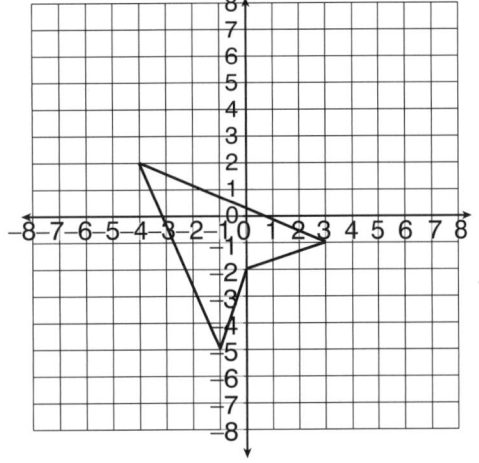

This graph shows the number of boys and girls in a school with birthdays in each month.

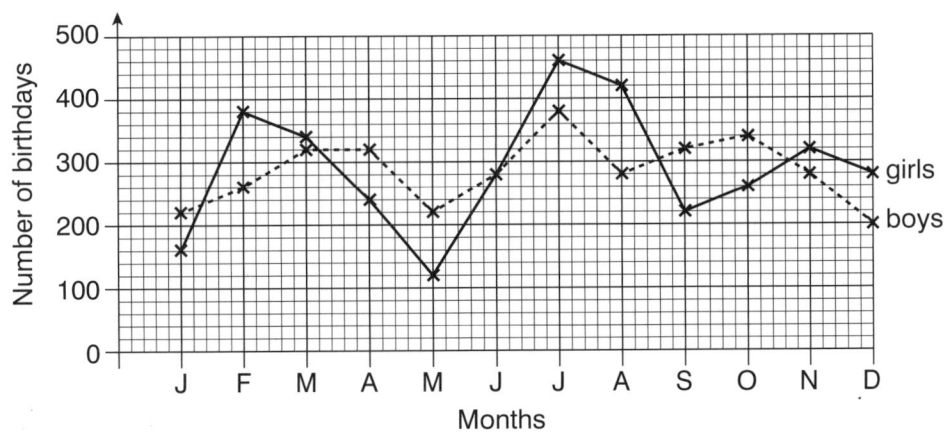

43 To the nearest 10, approximately how many girls were born in April?

_____

44 In which month were the same number of girls and boys born?

_____

45 How many more boys than girls were born in September?

_____

46 In which month is the difference in number of births between girls and boys the greatest? _____

These 1–9 digit cards are shuffled and placed face down in a row.

[3] [5] [8] [6] [4] [7] [1] [9] [2]

47 Underline the likelihood of picking a number less than 2.

impossible   poor chance   even chance   good chance   certain

48 Underline the likelihood of picking an odd number.

impossible   poor chance   even chance   good chance   certain

49 Underline the likelihood of picking a zero.

impossible   poor chance   even chance   good chance   certain

50 Which digit card is the median? _____

4

Now go to the Progress Chart to record your score!   Total   50

Mixed paper 7

Look at the table below, which shows the number of people who went on each ride at the funfair over a 12-month period.

RIDE	NUMBER OF PEOPLE
Rocky Roller Coaster	897 529
Orbiter Wheel	674 586
Tunnel of Terror	591 643
Dodgem Boats	305 886
Drop Tower	691 063

1–2 The Orbiter Wheel had how many people, rounded to the nearest 10 000? _____

How many people is this, rounded to the nearest 1000? _____

3–4 The Drop Tower had how many people, rounded to the nearest 100 000? _____

How many people is this, rounded to the nearest 100? _____

5–6 Which two rides together had the same number of people as the most popular ride? _____ , _____

7–8 What was the total number of people who went on the rides? _____

How many people is this to the nearest ten? _____

9–11 Write the missing numbers on this subtraction grid.

−	12.376	21.2
5.94		15.26
8.683		

12 Which 3 **prime** numbers under 15 multiply to make 165?

____ × ____ × ____ = 165

13 A right-angled isosceles triangle has two angles that are equal. What is the size of each angle? ____°

14–15 Circle the two numbers that are a multiple of 8.

84   96   108   128   133   142

16–17 Write the missing pair of factors for 92.

(1, 92)   (____, ____)   (4, 23)

18 What percentage of this grid is light grey? _____

19 What fraction of this grid is dark grey? _____

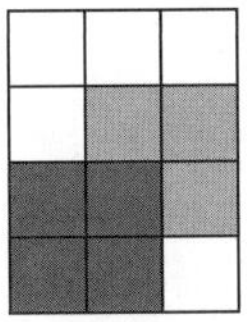

20 Write < or > to make this number sentence true.

2.35 ____ $2\frac{3}{5}$

21 There are 30 children in Class R and 18 are girls. What percentage of the class are girls? ____%

22 What is the missing number in this sequence? Circle the correct answer.

          40   50   70   100   ____   190

a 110 **b** 120 **c** 130 **d** 140

23–24 Write the missing numbers in this sequence.

    16   25   36   ____   64   ____   100   121

25 Write the next number in this sequence.

    0   1   3   6   10   15   ____

26–29 Write the letter for each of these in the correct part of this Carroll diagram.

A cuboid   B cylinder   C tetrahedron   D triangular prism

	1 or more rectangular faces	No rectangular faces
1 or more triangular faces	____	____
No triangular faces	____	____

This is the plan of a house in a garden.

30 What is the area of the house? _____ m²

31 What is the area of the garden, not including the area of the house? _____ m²

House 8m × 12m; Garden 30m × 15m

32 A fence will be put round the whole garden. The fence panels are 1.5 m wide. How many fence panels will be needed? ____ fence panels

33 Draw a rectangle with an area of 64 squares and a perimeter of 40 squares.

34 Write the total length of these two bricks in millimetres. _____ mm

35 What is the total length of five bricks? _____ cm

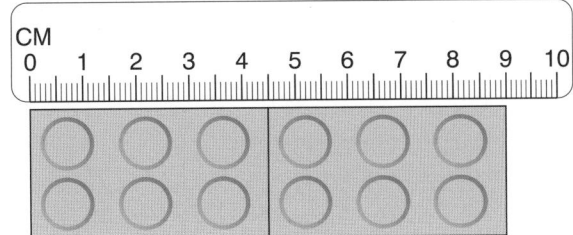

Each of these parcels weighs a different amount.

Parcel B and C weigh 7 kg together.

Parcel A is double the weight of parcel B.

The total weight of all three parcels is 15 kg.

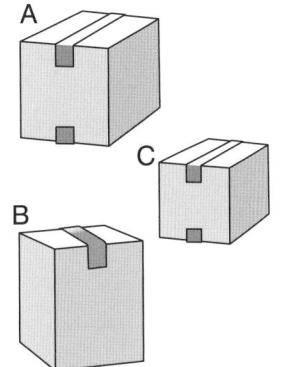

36 What is the weight of parcel A? _____ kg
37 What is the weight of parcel B? _____ kg
38 What is the weight of Parcel C? _____ kg

39 This triangle has been rotated to make a pattern. Draw the next rotation in this sequence.

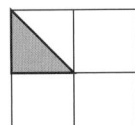 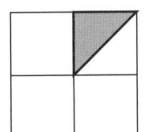 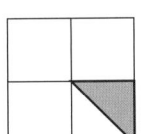 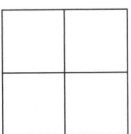

40 This is a rectangle. Write in the missing coordinates. (_____, _____)

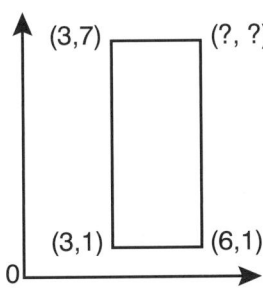

41 These shapes show a **reflection**. Draw the mirror line that these shapes have been reflected in.

42 Circle the coordinates that are **not** on the mirror line.

(4, 4)   (3, −3)   (−2, −2)   (0, 0)

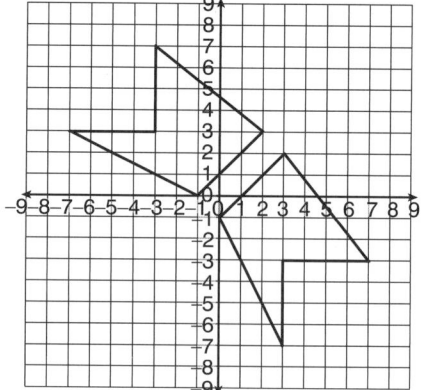

This pie chart shows what Kate did with £10 of pocket money.

43 How much did Kate save? _____

44 How much did she spend on the boat ride? _____

45 How much did she spend on sweets? _____

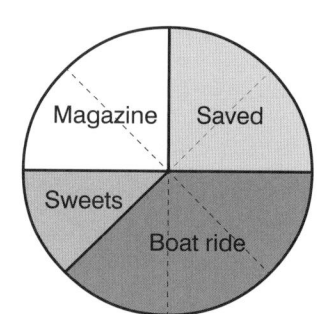

46 How much did she spend in total? _____

47 If the mean of two numbers is 8 and one number is 9, what is the other number? _____

48 The total marks in a science test were 512. If the mean mark was 32, how many children took the test? _____

49 If the probability is 0.4 that it will not rain tomorrow, what is the probability that it will rain tomorrow? _____

50 Write the probability, expressed as a percentage, of flipping 'heads' on a coin. _____

Now go to the Progress Chart to record your score!   Total   50

Mixed paper 8

1–4 Write this set of decimals in order to make this number sentence correct.

6.024   4.602   4.604   6.246

_____ < _____ < _____ < _____

5-7 The letters A, B and C stand for three even numbers from 1–9. Using the grid below, work out which number each letter represents.

	C	A	B
	C	B	B
+	B	C	B
1	7	3	2

A = 2   B = 4   C = 6

8 Divide one hundred and eighty-three point six by zero point three. __612__

9-10 Three parcels weigh 8.1 kg. One parcel weighs 3.5 kg and the other two parcels have a difference of 1 kg. Complete the missing weights of the other two parcels.

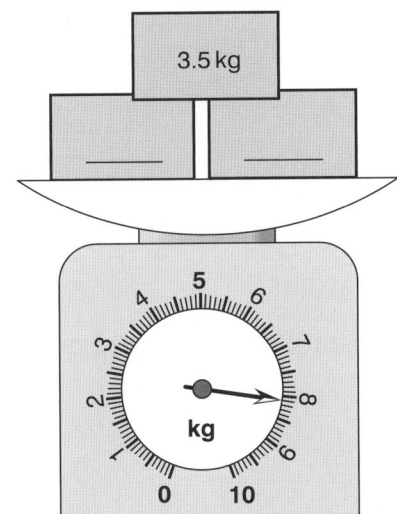

11 Which number between 60 and 70 has a remainder of 5 when it is divided by 8? __61__

12 Eggs are sold in boxes of 12. A farmer collects 78 eggs in one day. How many egg boxes can be completely filled? __6__

13 I am thinking of a number. I divide it by 7 and then multiply it by 50 and my answer is 450. What is my number? __63__

14 A bag of potatoes weighs 2.5 kg. A supermarket shelf can hold a maximum weight of 30 kg. How many bags of potatoes can this shelf hold? __12__

Are these statements true or false? Circle the correct answer.

15 A multiple of 9 is always an odd number. True / False

16 When the digits of a number that is a multiple of 9 are added together, that total will always have 9 as a factor. True / False

17 The number 30 has a total of 6 factors. True / False

18 A square number always has an odd number of factors. True / False

19–20 Circle the two cards that show more than $\frac{1}{2}$

8% $\frac{3}{8}$ 0.8   0.35 $\frac{3}{5}$ 38%

21 Abinaath spends $\frac{3}{8}$ of his money on a game, $\frac{2}{5}$ of his money on a T-shirt and $\frac{1}{10}$ of his money on lunch. He has £12 left. How much money did he have to start with? _____

The Village Bakery spends 33% of its weekly budget for ingredients on flour. It spends 15% on sugar and 28% on butter. The remaining budget is spent on dried fruit, which costs £48.

22 How much money is spent on flour? _____

23 How much money is spent on butter? _____

24 How much money is spent on sugar? _____

25–26 The rule for this sequence is to multiply the number by 3. Write the missing numbers in this sequence.

2.4   _____   21.6   64.8   _____

27–28 Write the missing numbers in this sequence.

_____   2010   2310   2610   2910   _____

Look at this square.

29 Without using a protractor calculate the angle marked x. _____

30 Which line is parallel to line AB? _____

31 What type of triangle is ABD? _____

32 Write **always**, **sometimes** or **never** to make this sentence true.

A cube _____ has 2 square faces and 4 rectangle faces.

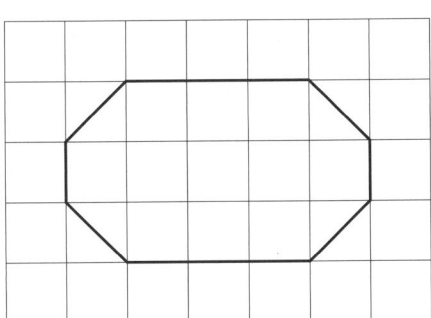

33 Calculate the area of the shape on this 1 cm square grid.
_____ cm²

34 A rectangular lawn measures 7.5 m by 4 m. A packet of 'Seed and Feed' is enough for 15 m². How many packets of 'Seed and Feed' would be needed for this lawn? _____

Calculate the area and perimeter of this shape.

35 Area = _____ cm²

36 Perimeter = _____ cm

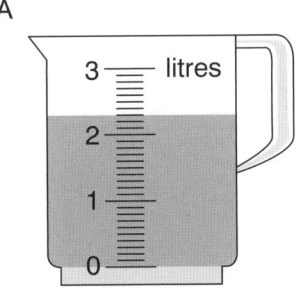

37 What is the difference, in millilitres, between the amount of water in these two jugs? _____ ml

38 If these two jugs of water were poured together, how much **more** water would be needed to fill a 5 litre bowl? Write your answer in millilitres. _____ ml

Enter <, > or = to make each statement true.

39 40.5 cm _____ 405 mm   **40** 180 g _____ 1.8 kg

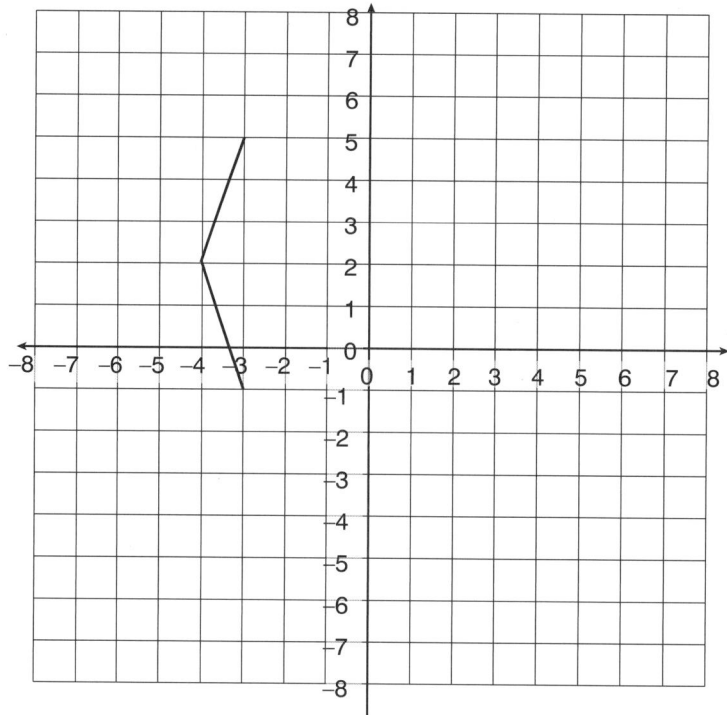

41 Mark coordinates (0, −2) on the grid. This is the fourth vertex of a quadrilateral. Draw two lines to complete this shape.

42 Draw a reflection of this shape, using the *y*-axis as the line of symmetry. Write the missing three coordinates of the reflected shape.

(0, −2) (____, ____) (____, ____) (____, ____)

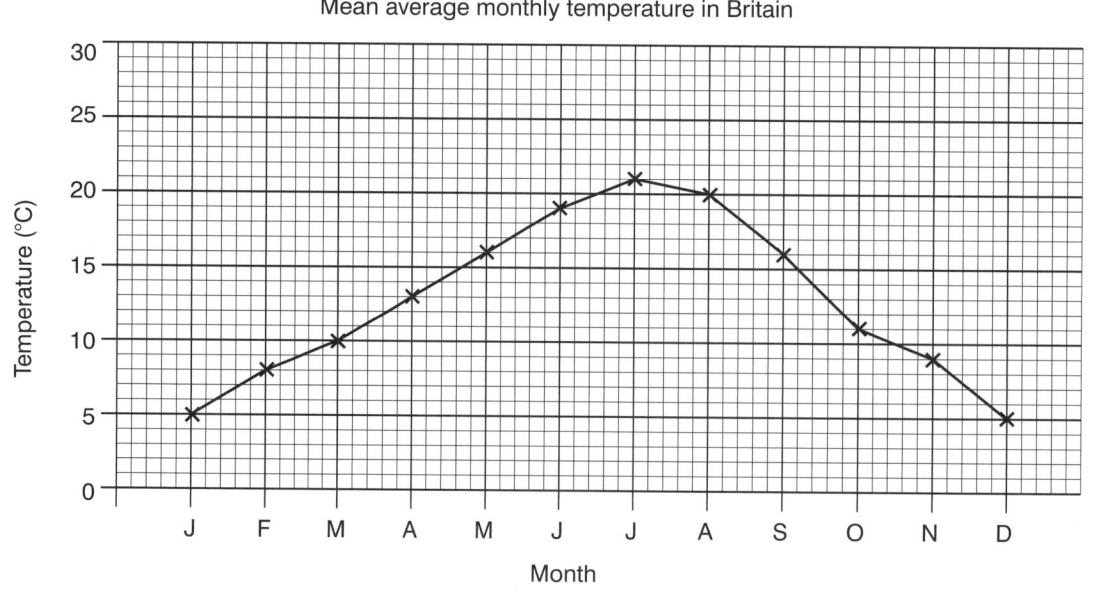

54

43 Which month has a mean temperature of 10°C? _____

44 What is the mean temperature in April? _____

45 Which month has the same mean temperature as September? _____

46 What is the difference in temperature between the coldest month and the hottest month? _____

47 June, July and August are the summer months. What is the mean temperature for the whole summer? _____

48 December, January and February are the winter months. What is the mean temperature for the whole winter? _____

49 What is the mean temperature for the whole year? _____

50 What is the median temperature for the whole year? _____

Now go to the Progress Chart to record your score! Total 50